*Babel Guides* are a unique and original series of guides to a country's writing; reviewing and listing books available in English.

This *Babel Guide* presents modern Brazilian fiction: novels, short-story collections and anthologies translated into English. In addition to the database of translations at the end, many individual works are reviewed. Each review is followed by a brief extract, to give a flavour of the book.

# The Babel Guide to Brazilian Fiction in English Translation

by David Treece & Ray Keenoy

*with*

David Brookshaw, Aviva Cohen, Marina Coriolano-Lykourezos, Maria Amelia Dalsenter, Stephanie Dennison, Angela Dierks, John Gledson, Robert Howes, Tom MacCarthy, Nancy Naro, Giovanni Pontiero, Siobhan Smith, Sean Stroud and Claire Williams

**BOULEVARD**

Babel Guide to Brazilian Fiction
©Boulevard Books 2001
First published 2001 by Boulevard Books
71 Lytton Road
Oxford OX4 3NY, UK
Tel/Fax 01865 712931
email: raybabel@dircon.co.uk


This project was aided by the Lei de incentivo à cultura of the Ministério de cultura, Brazil, FAAP and Brazil 500. The publisher would like to thank the cultural staff and officials of the Brazilian Embassy, London for their help and encouragement and Dr. David Treece for his long-standing *khavershaft*.


ISBN 1-899460-70-5

Boulevard Books are distributed in the **UK & Europe** by Drake International, Market House, Market Place, Deddington, Oxford OX15 0SE tel 01869 338240 fax 338310 info@drakeint.co.uk www.drakeint.co.uk and in the **USA & Canada** by ISBS 5804 NE Hassio St, Portland, Oregon 97213-3644 tel 00 1 503 287 3093 fax 280 8832 info@isbs.com


Cover Art: Jackie Wrout
Typeset & Design: Studio Europa
Printed and bound by Intype, Wimbledon, London

| | |
|---|---|
| 11 | Auhors and anthologies reviewed |
| 13 | Reviews of selected books |
| 140 | Reviews of Anthologies |
| 149 | Contributors |
| 151 | Brazilian Fiction translated into English Database |

## Authors and Anthologies reviewed

ABREU
Caio Fernando
ALENCAR
José de
ALMEIDA
José Américo de
ALMEIDA
Manuel Antônio de
AMADO
Jorge
ANDRADE
Mário de
ANJOS
Cyro dos
AZEVEDO
Aluizio de
BUARQUE
Chico
CALLADO
Antônio
CAMINHA
Adolfo
CÉSAR
Ana Cristina
COELHO
Paulo
CUNHA
Euclides da
CUNHA
Helena Parente
DOURADO
Autran
FELINTO
Marilene
FONSECA
Rubem
GALVÃO
Patrícia
GAMA
José Basílio da
GUIMARÃES ROSA
João
HATOUM
Milton
LIMA BARRETO
Afonso Henriques
LISPECTOR
Clarice
LUFT
Lya
MACHADO DE ASSIS
Joaquim Maria
MELO
Patricia
MIRANDA
Ana
NOLL
João Gilberto
OLINTO
Antonio
PIÑON
Nélida
QUEIROZ
Rachel de
RAMOS
Graciliano
RIBEIRO
Darcy
RIBEIRO
João Ubaldo
SCLIAR
Moacyr
SOUZA
Márcio
VEIGA
José J.
VERÍSSIMO
Érico

ANTHOLOGY
Caistor, N.(Ed.)
Faber Book of Contemporary Latin American Short Stories
ANTHOLOGY
Grossman, W. (Ed.)
Modern Brazilian Short Stories
ANTHOLOGY
Darlene J. Sadlier (Ed. and translator)
One Hundred Years After Tomorrow: Brazilian Women's Fiction in the 20th Century
ANTHOLOGY
Cristina Ferreira-Pinto (ed.)
Urban Voices. Contemporary Short Stories from Brazil

# ABREU
Caio Fernando

## Dragons [Os dragões não conhecem o paraíso]

There's a strange familiarity about the stories of *Dragons*... Not the familiarity of something we feel we've read or heard spoken before — although the sensation of déjà-vu, the bittersweet memory or echo of emotions felt in some other time, somewhere else, by someone else, is experienced on many occasions in the pages of this book, by the characters — and by the reader. Nor am I simply talking about the 'punks, beggars, neon lights, prostitutes and moaning synthesizers' that float about in the night fog of the story entitled 'The Saddest Boy in the World', the health freaks and wind surfers of 'Blues Without Ana', the unfulfilled, slightly ageing professional couple looking for romance second time around in a phoney tropical holiday resort, in 'Honey and Sunflowers'. Of course all these social types help remind us that not only the physical landscapes, but the human landscapes, too, of London, New York, Tokyo and São Paulo are growing more alike as we enter the last decade of the twentieth century.

But more than these things, it's the familiarity of recognition, the recognition of experiences that have been or at least could be our own: a young boy's struggle to come to terms with his awakening adolescent sexuality; the joyful discovery of shared emotions and sensations; the pain and the anger of separation; the exhilaration and danger of freedom; the panic and grief of loneliness. They are experiences which have been moulded, made theirs and ours, by the common conditions of our global culture in the 1990s, a culture of uncertainty, decay and alienation, in which the traditional models of social, economic and family life have failed to provide happiness and security for the majority, while at the same time repressing or excluding those who have discovered alternative sexual identities and lifestyles. It's a culture, too, which continually sells us a thousand ready-made mass-produced roles and masks, offering us instant identity in an anonymous world, the identity of the cliché, the stereotype, allowing us to forget who we really are, if we ever knew. These are the lost souls who inhabit the pages of *Dragons;*

'The Totally Liberated But Profoundly Misunderstood Woman Who Accepted Her Inevitable Solitude, the Independent Man Who Can Do Without That Nonsense Called Love, the Psychoanalyst At Odds with the Elitism of Her Own Profession, or the Basketball Player Looking for a More Natural Life.'

This sense of familiarity or recognition, even if it is the recognition of our shared anonymity, alienation and marginalisation, is extremely important, particularly when our perceptions of Latin America and Latin Americans have been largely shaped by a literature which emphasizes their *difference* from us, their uniqueness and the impossibility of understanding their world. With one or two exceptions, European and North American publishers have until recently preferred to publish those Latin American (and occasionally Brazilian) authors whose work confirms the image of an exotic, alien, incomprehensible culture, whose essence lies in its magical 'primitiveness', its pre-industrial, pre-capitalist backwardness, its 'Third-Worldness'. The publication of this book in English contributes towards a new understanding of the experience of those living in Latin America, and Brazil in particular.

In that sense, for all the familiarity of the dramas told to us by Caio, they are also profoundly Latin American. The emotions of self-discovery, loss, bewilderment and despair have an extra intensity that has something to do with the special impact of our global crisis on the cities of Buenos Aires, Lima, São Paulo and Rio de Janeiro. The lateness, swiftness and brutality of modernisation in these places, their lack of any control over the process, and their fragility and weakness in the face of the world's major economic powers, all these things have made the lives of the newly urbanised Latin American masses especially traumatic and alienated. How many of Caio's characters are found drifting in a limbo between the provincial towns of their childhood and the faceless metropolis? Like the narrator of *A Little White Sandy Beach, Down by the Gully* who says:

'...that's what happens when you leave a little town that's stopped being yours and go and live in another town that hasn't started being yours yet. You always start feeling a bit weird when you think you don't really want to stay but you don't want to — or can't — go back either. You feel just like one of those guys in the circus who walks the tightrope and suddenly the wire breaks, snap! and you're just hanging there, suspended in mid-air, empty space below your feet. With nowhere in the world to go, do you know what I mean?'

If the masks and roles we take on are already borrowed ready-made from the fictional world of advertising or the soap opera, then the illusion becomes a double-deception for a culture whose role models are imported from Dallas or Hollywood. How much more difficult it is to sustain the dream of True Love in one of the biggest AIDS capitals of the world, where state health care is virtually non-existent, and, as the young kid in 'The Queen of the Night' hears, the telly tells you 'love kills love kills love kills'?

It's all the more moving and inspiring, then, to witness Caio's characters struggling, against all these odds, to find love, to peer through the fog, reach out and touch, and even, occasionally to celebrate the innocence of a shared moment of warmth and communication recovered from a filthy, corrupted world. Sometimes all that is possible in a fragmented, atomised society such as this, is the continuity and meaning offered by the mystical language of astral coincidences, Chinese horoscopes or the symbolism of candomblé. At other times, the characters have nothing to cling to but the dependable, eternal image of a matinée idol, or the dream of an invisible dragon. It is these courageous struggles that we have the privilege of witnessing when we read the stories of Caio Fernando Abreu, stories which invite, not just sympathy or comprehension but recognition and solidarity. DT

When Ana left me, I stood for a long time in the living room of the apartment with her note in my hands. It was around eight o'clock in the evening. The clocks were on summer time and through the open living-room window it was still possible to make out, in that eight o'clock in the evening light, a few traces of gold and red left by the sun going down behind the buildings over towards Pinheiros. I stood there a long time, in the middle of the living room, Ana's last note in my hands, looking out of the window at the reds and golds in the sky. And I remember thinking, 'now the phone's going to ring': it might have been Lucinha ringing from the agency or Paulo from the film club or Nelson from Paris or my mother from the South, inviting me to dinner, to snort some coke, to see Nastassia Kinski in the nude, asking what the weather was like or something like that, but it didn't ring so after some time in which it hadn't rung I thought, 'now someone's going to ring the doorbell'. It might be the janitor delivering some mail, the neighbour from upstairs looking for her Persian cat that liked to escape down the stairs... But the doorbell didn't ring either, and I stood there for a good while longer without any means of salvation, in the middle of the room which was beginning to turn a bluish colour as the evening drew on, like the inside of a fish tank, Ana's note in my hands, doing absolutely nothing except breathe. 30–31

## ABREU
Caio Fernando

### Whatever happened to Dulce Veiga?: a B-novel [Onde andará Dulce Veiga?]

Caio Fernando Abreu's 'B-novel' takes you on a roller coaster ride around the underground literary and pop world of nocturnal São Paulo. The novel's nameless protagonist, a disillusioned forty year-old journalist, is on the trail of the ever elusive Dulce Veiga, a famous singer who mysteriously disappeared twenty years earlier. On his search for Dulce our down-trodden hero comes across a medley of fortune-tellers, gay Pietàs, junkies, transvestites, revolutionaries, Afro-Brazilian gods and rock stars, all set against the background of a decrepit metropolis full of dilapidated buildings and overflowing rubbish bins.

*Whatever happened to Dulce Veiga?* has all the hallmarks of a hard-boiled detective novel: a cynical hero, a mystery, a glamorous, missing singer, various characters who all seem to know more than the protagonist does, and a slowly unravelling plot. Yet it is also a novel about the protagonist's journey of self-discovery. His quest for Dulce, who appears to him in a variety of situations, each of them like a revelation, triggers off suppressed memories not only of a first meeting with Dulce but also the protagonist's first gay lover, Pedro. The latter mirrors Dulce in disappearing suddenly from his life. They are the polar opposites that shape the tensions in the protagonist's sexual life — femme fatale versus gay god.

The novel is multi-layered, combining three storylines: the narrator's present search for Dulce, his memories of a first meeting with Dulce and his memories of his lost lover. All these different strands finally merge on a metaphysical level with the protagonist finding his identity and peace, aptly being called by his name for the first time. The physical setting for the narrator's spiritual rebirth is Estrela do Norte, a magical town that would be familiar to viewers of Walter Salles' hugely successful film *Central Station*, where the two main characters similarly reach the end of their quest.

Caio Fernando Abreu's 'B-Novel' is post-modern in its cultural references to film, art, TV and music; in fact most of the rather loud characters could feature in an over-the-top soap opera set amongst São Paulo's bohemia. Above all, *Whatever happened to Dulce Veiga?* is also an intensely funny novel that will provoke regular fits of chuckling.
A D

On the overpass, the beggar put down the bag of paper. Then, with both hands free, and a gesture that was too elegant for her, she took off her hood. She had blond, straight hair parted in the middle and cut at chin level. She held her arm up, her forefinger pointing to the sky, and turned her face toward me. Even filthy and with a scabby nose, her face still showed traces of its past beauty.
I cried:
'Dulce, wait for me, Dulce Veiga!'
I started running with the bottle in my hand. The Portuguese guy shouted something I didn't catch. I lost sight of her for a moment, until I managed

to cross the street, go around the concrete island under the overpass, and run up toward her. Ah, I'd take her home, give her a bath, get her to tell me all the obscure details of that crazy story, then we'd go to the opening of Márcia's show together. Happy ending: in the back, Dulce would sing 'Nothing More' beneath a deluge of roses and applause. In the forefront, Márcia and I holding hands, gazing into each other's eyes. Credits rolling over the freeze-frame.

But we weren't there yet, it wasn't like that yet. 116

# ALENCAR
José de

## Iracema [Iracema]

One of the most frequently read of the Brazilian classics, perhaps the best known literary title in the country, the Indianist prose-poem *Iracema* is a 'foundational romance' about the colonial birth-pangs of the nation. Published in 1865, at the height of the Romantic Indianist movement, it formed part of a project to fictionalise the totality of Brazil's early and contemporary history — something like Balzac's *Comédie Humaine* — undertaken by the country's most important novelist before Machado de Assis: José de Alencar. As well as its extravagant lyrical language — Alencar's pseudo-indigenous phraseology and vocabulary got a hostile reception from contemporary purists — the main innovation *Iracema* brought to the Indianist tradition was its depiction of a 'marriage', albeit a tragic one, between a Portuguese soldier and a *tabajara* tribeswoman, who gives birth to the country's archetypal, 'first' mixed-race son.

Alencar was the first writer to propose miscegenation, the idea of national identity and unity built upon a colonial legacy of *mestiços*, (people of mixed Amerindian and European descent) as a fictional means of papering over the huge contradictions left untouched by Brazil's independence from Portugal, not least that of black slavery (Afro-Brazilians did not enter his interracial equation at all). And while the regional scenario of Alencar's native province, Ceará, and certain principal characters in the novel, such as the military commander and colonist Martim Afonso and his Potiguara Indian ally Antonio Felipe Camarão, are drawn from the history of early conquest and settlement in the Northeast of the country, this is not a historical novel as such. For here the violence of conquest, the sexual as well as military subjugation of the indigenous population, becomes mythologised as a pre-eminently erotic affair, a 'fatal attraction', responsibility for which is shouldered implicitly by both parties. The seduction — in which

Martim persuades the priestess of the tribe to break her holy vows, only to discover that during his drug-induced dream of sexual possession Iracema has actually joined him in the hammock — involves duplicity, guilt, irresponsibility and betrayal in equal shares.

Alencar was not such an idealist as to believe that a marriage on these foundations could last — now that Martim's fantasy of the dark-skinned exotic temptress has lost her virginal charm, he prefers the male company of his fellow warriors, while the clinging, all self-sacrificing Iracema inexorably fades away in her grief-stricken abandonment. His rather more subtle point was that their mixed-race son, Moacyr, will survive the mother of the nation, free to live out his life as neither Indian nor colonist but as a true Brazilian, obliged to acknowledge his parents' sacrifices and failings yet also leave them behind him, to remember but never to avenge them.

In this sense Alencar was giving his nineteenth-century bourgeois readers, with their liberal pretensions yet their determination not to relinquish the benefits of slavery, just what they needed: a fantasy that could allow them to come to terms with their history without contemplating the need for change. After reading this extraordinarily lyrical narrative with its accumulation of metaphors and similes linking the characters' inner and outer lives to the endless cycles of nature, it is difficult to resist Alencar's own, literary seduction, the illusion that the tragedies of human history are as natural and inevitable as the falling away of the leaves from the jacaranda tree. DT

The arms of the sleeping warrior opened, and his lips; the maiden's name was gently intoned.

The juriti, wandering through the forest, hears the tender cooing of its mate; it beats its wings and flies to find shelter in its warm nest. So did the maiden of the interior nestle in the warrior's arms.

When morning came, it still found Iracema enfolded there, like a butterfly that has slept in the bosom of the shapely cactus. On her lovely countenance, abashment had kindled a vivid scarlet, and like the first ray of sun glittering among the red clouds of morning, on her burning cheeks shone a wife's first smile, the dawn of a love come to fruition.

The jandaia had flown with the break of day, never to return to the hut.

Seeing the maiden united to his heart, Martim thought he was still dreaming; he closed his eyes and reopened them.

The warriors' battle cry, reverberating through the valley, plucked him from the sweet error: he sensed he was no longer dreaming, but living. His cruel hand stifled on the maiden's lips the kiss that fluttered there.

'Iracema's kisses are sweet in dreams; the white warrior has filled his soul with them. In life, the lips of Tupã's virgin are bitter and wound like the jurema thorn.'

Araquém's daughter concealed the happiness in her heart. She became shy and restless, like the bird that foresees the tempest on the horizon. She moved quickly away and departed.

The waters of the river bathed the chaste body of the new bride.

Tupã no longer had his virgin in the land of the Tabajaras. 50–51

# ALMEIDA
José Américo de

## Trash [A Bagaceira]

First published in 1928, *Trash* represents a landmark in Brazilian literature, as it was the first truly regionalist Brazilian novel of the type which had already appeared in other parts of Latin America. So great was its impact that the critic Tristão de Athayde declared that its publication divided the twentieth-century Brazilian novel into two groups; those that came before, and those that followed. By breaking new literary ground, *Trash* opened the way for a crop of influential novels such as Rachel de Queiroz's *O Quinze* (1930), José Lins de Rego's *Menino de Engenho* (1932), Jorge Amado's *Cacau* (1933), and Graciliano Ramos's *São Bernardo* (1934), all of which reflected a new-found desire to portray the lives of the inhabitants of Brazil's largely neglected interior, rather than those of the urban centres of Rio de Janeiro and São Paulo. With its stylistic innovations, such as the use of typically Brazilian Portuguese, its terse, almost documentary narrative, and its vibrant depiction of the flora and fauna of the *sertão* (backlands) and the *brejo* (lowlands), the novel represented a rejection of the often florid literary stylings which preceded it.

Almeida's tale of thwarted love, revenge, and inter-regional conflict in the northeast may strike the contemporary reader as slightly implausible and sensationalist in tone, yet his stark depiction of the apocalyptic effects of the periodic droughts which plague the region still packs a powerful punch.

Almeida compares the conditions of the refugees from drought with those scratching out a precarious living as workers at the sugar mill owned by a local landowner named Dagoberto. The pitiful plight of these workers is related in graphic detail by the author as he describes the dehumanising conditions within the mill in which they toil, with no legal protection from their exploitative boss. Dagoberto's death leaves the way clear for his more socially aware son, Lúcio, to take over the mill. Yet despite Lúcio's determination to modernise the methods of production at the mill and his genuine intentions to care for his workers, he is conscious that by treating them with dignity he has ironically created the conditions for their own eventual emancipation. SS

It was the exodus from the drought of 1898 — a resurrection from ancient cemeteries of resuscitated skeletons of claylike appearance and stinking of the charnel house. Emaciated ghosts, their shaky, unsteady steps seemed like a dance as they dragged themselves along in the manner of one who is carrying his legs instead of being carried by them. They walked slowly, looking back behind them as if anxious to return. There was no hurry to arrive, for none knew where he was going. Expelled from their paradise by swords of flame, tormented by furies, they wandered aimlessly on, fleeing the sun, their guide in this enforced nomadism.

  Wasted to a comical thinness they seemed to be supported by the wind, while from skinny arms their hands hung loosely below their knees.

  They carried no bundles. All, except for those sick from eating poisonous plants, had hugely distended bellies. They possessed neither age nor sex nor any distinguishing feature. They were refugees. Nothing more. 14

## ALMEIDA
Manuel Antônio de

### Memoirs of a Militia Sergeant [Memórias de um sargento de milícias]

What did it mean to be free, but poor, in a country of masters and slaves? Almeida's novel, first serialised in 1852, gives us a fascinating and highly entertaining glimpse into the lives of Rio de Janeiro's 'middling folk' — barbers and midwives, policemen and schoolteachers, palace servants and petty legal functionaries, gypsies and sorcerers — at the beginning of the nineteenth century. In fact, we could say that the novel, set in the period between 1808 and 1821, when the Portuguese court took flight from the threat of Napoleon's armies and installed itself in Brazil's future capital, bears witness to the birth of the modern city, one with an entire way of life, a 'popular culture', that was unique to those sandwiched between the country's ruling and producing classes, and who were forced to survive by their own wits and means.

  One of a kind, it's impossible to pigeonhole this book in any of the literary movements of the century: too sketchy and narrow in its social focus to be a Realist novel, but too morally neutral and anti-idealist to be a Romantic work. The rough and tumble of the young rogue Leonardo's adventures, and his transit through a succession of precarious 'positions' before his eventual marriage and enlistment in the militia, make comparisons with picaresque novels like *Tom Jones* or *Lazarillo de Tormes* tempting. But here the blows of life are always cushioned for Leonardo by an entire network of mutual support — kinship relations, sponsorship, favours, surrogate families (from which the mythical Brazilian patriarch seems conspicuously absent) — that allow him to enjoy rather than suffer his condition of congenital vagrancy, a 'dependent' on the good will and hospitality of those around him. So the pace of the book is set not so much by the drama of social ascendancy and success against the odds, as by Leonardo's endless, playful efforts to evade the career plans laid by his concerned sponsors and to outwit the forces of officialdom, law and order, epitomised above all by the terrifying character of the chief of police, Major Vidigal (based on a actual historical figure).

All of this confirms the view of Brazil's leading literary critic, Antonio Candido, that Leonardo represents a prototype of that icon of Brazilian popular lowlife who became legendary following the abolition of slavery, in the first half of the twentieth century: the *malandro* or hustler who, by a mixture of cunning and charm manages to dance his way along a tight-rope between the world of respectability and power, and that of poverty and humiliation. In Almeida's indulgence of Leonardo's cheeky indolence and of the general irreverence of Rio society towards officialdom (the novel includes some wonderful little vignettes of religious festivals that have been hijacked and 'carnivalised' by the people), it is the satirical journalist's eye for the truth that comes through, his determination to tear away the veil of polite hypocrisy and tell it as it really was. This makes the book a refreshing and rare alternative to the mainstream literature of the period, with its myths and romances of the new-born nation. A real gem, one of Oxford University Press's excellent new Library of Latin America series, accompanied by two informative and enlightening essays on the novel and its context. DT

'Here comes the weasel now, Major.'

'Close in, close in!' said the major.

And each man went off to his assigned position. The major hid in a corridor doorway and kept his eye out.

There approached the major a figure calmly whistling the refrain of a *modinha*. When he was a short distance away the major leaped out at him and seized him.

A feeble 'ay' was uttered, accompanied by a 'Release me! What is this?'

The major looked more closely, since he had not recognised the voice of Teotônio, and saw that he had captured a poor hunchback, one who on top of that was crippled in the right leg and the left arm...
The major burned with a fury and, gathering together the grenadiers, said to Leonardo: 'He didn't come out —'
'Yes, he did,' the latter replied; 'wearing a white jacket and a straw hat. I saw him turn down toward the door where you were posted.'
'White jacket and straw hat?' asked the major.
'Yes, sir, and black breeches. I didn't grab him because I could see that he wasn't going to be able to escape you, Major, sir.'
'Oh the scoundrel, the scoundrel,' he muttered. 'I've never been so... It was the hunchback, the cripple...'
'He does a very good hunchback and a very good cripple,' said one of the grenadiers. 'I saw him do them once, and it was just like real life...'
The cripple the major had captured had indeed been Teotônio. Leonardo laughed up his sleeve at the trick that had been played on the major.

It was not long, however, before that pleasure turned sour, as the major came to find out that it had all been done with his connivance.
152–53

## AMADO
Jorge

### Captains of the Sand [Capitães da areia]

*Captains of the Sand* is a fine book from Amado's early more politically and socially focused period of work and was first published in Brazil in 1937. Seventy-odd years later it becomes a book with a new relevance — as a lively portrait of a gang of 'street children', now seen as a rising social problem in Latin America's cities. It is clear from Amado's sympathetic and well-thought out narrative that this is not a new problem: children were already detaching themselves from, or being abandoned by, fractured families existing in such precariousness that even minimal care for children was impossible.

Although there is a documentary intent in *Captains of the Sand* its romantic title already suggests that Amado wanted to create a lyrical, 'legendary' form for his story of a group of abandoned, mainly Black, children in Salvador da Bahia in North-Eastern Brazil. Amado's legend is linked in with the legendary bandit Lampião, a backlands Robin Hood, reminding us that fashionable 'Afro' Bahia has, like Brazil in general, a large hinterland of maltreated peasants and labourers, whose heroes have often been 'social bandits' like Lampião.

The boys of the 'Captains of the Sand' gang, so-called because they live on the silted-up waterfront where sailing ships used to dock, are described with lyricism: although the victims of political and economic harshness Amado encloses them within the (culturally) rich world of Afro-Bahia. Especially at the time of writing this celebration of Black and 'syncretic' (i.e. the mixing of European, Indian and African religious and cultural elements as practised in Brazil) culture was scandalous: below the surface the book seethes with its black priestess mãe-de-santo, the Yoruba Gods Xangô and Ogun and the Sea-Goddess Iemanjá. Apart though from letting us in on something of the famous candomblé syncretic religion of Bahia, Amado stresses that this little gang of thieves are children, with tender, wounded hearts, who have been forced into crime and not the squad of delinquents and monsters that the police, newspapers and establishment see them as.

The format of *Captains of the Sand* is episodic with illustrative micro-stories within its longer narrative and Amado also uses a pastiche technique with cod newspaper articles and letters. This reflects literary experiments of the 1920s and 30s such as the work of John Dos Passos in the US. One of the best of the little narrative tracks is the story of the carousel when the captains take over a battered merry-go-round. Amado's description of the children's harsh joy in it demonstrates one of the reasons for his immense popularity in Brazil and the rest of the world; his ability to evoke and share pleasures with us, whether childish or, as often in his work, less innocent sexual ones. RK

The 'Great Japanese Carrousel' was nothing but a small native merry-go-round that arrived after a sad pilgrimage through inland towns during those winter months when the rains are long and Christmas is still far off. So faded was the paint, paint that had once been blue and red, that the blue was a dirty white now and the red was almost pink, and so many pieces were missing on certain horses and benches that Nhôzinho França decided not to set it up in any of the main squares of the city but in Itapagipe. The families there aren't so rich, there are a lot of streets where only workers live, and poor children would appreciate the faded old carrousel... It had been beautiful once, it had even been the pride and joy of the children of Maceió in other days. At that time it stood alongside a Ferris wheel and a side-show, always on the same square, and on Sundays and holidays rich children dressed in sailor suits or like little English lords, the girls in Dutch costumes or fine silk dresses, came to claim their favourite horses, the little ones sitting on the benches with their nannies. The fathers would go on the Ferris wheel, others preferred the side-show, where they could push up against women, often touching their thighs and buttocks. Nhôzinho França's carnival was the joy of the city in those days. 49

# AMADO
Jorge

## Dona Flor and her Two Husbands [Dona Flor e seus dois maridos]

Here is Amado's book of Bahian cuisine, with its African, tropical and coastal elements celebrated throughout Brazil. See for instance ; what to serve at a wake (p1), Dona Flor's recipe for marinated crabs (p14), stewed turtle and other unusual dishes (p221) and the culinary likes and dislikes of deities (p421).

The reader will not find a complete cookery book in this, one of Amado's most famous works, but might enjoy his recipe for an international best-seller. The story of the beautiful Dona Flor is set in the lush tropics of Bahia (on the North-East coast of Brazil). Flor marries Vadinho — gambler, bohemian, womaniser. Make him die, still young and charming, during the celebration of Carnival. Bring the story to a simmer in the tears of Dona Flor the widow, suffering from the tongues of the local gossips and from her own memories of pleasure and impossible desire. Add a new husband — with a degree, a pharmacy, some money, and complete devotion to his lovely new wife. When the narrative is about to fall into the boring rut of middle-class marriage, add the supernatural element that will give an exquisite flavour to the dish.

Undoubtedly, only Jorge Amado could season this everyday plot and turn it into a special dish of Bahian cuisine composed of humour, love, sex, friendship, bohemian life, social analysis and unforgettable characters. All of them are present in Amado's pages and in the streets of Bahia, in the 'fearsome battle between spirit and matter'. M-AD

I am the husband of the poor Dona Flor, the one who comes to stir up your longing and provoke your desire, hidden in the depths of your being, your modesty. He is the husband of Madame Dona Flor, who protects your virtue, your honour, your respect among people. He is your outward face, I your inner, the lover whom you don't know how and can't bear to evade. We are your two husbands, your two faces, your yes, your no. To be happy you need both of us. 535

# AMADO
## Jorge
### Gabriela, Clove and Cinnamon [Gabriela, cravo e canela]

'The Colonels will go crazy over her. But don't tell anybody that they're not married. Every colonel's fondest dream is to sleep with a married woman. Only, if anybody tries to sleep with *his* wife – oh boy!'.

If a man doesn't shoot his wife and her lover when he finds them in bed together he is run out of town in disgrace. If a man doesn't visit the cabarets and brothels it is generally concluded that something is really wrong with him. But if a woman doesn't remain faithful to her husband she ruins the family's name and honour. If a kept woman has another man, she is beaten and run out of town too. If a man wants something, he's got his henchmen. If there is a matter to discuss, both parties have their henchmen. Such is the state of affairs in Ilhéus, in southern Brazil, the cocoa capital. There is no need for complicated laws or political institutions. Things are very clearly defined in this society. It is a question of bullets not ballots.

In everything, loyalty is the key; it is what the whole social order rests on. A woman is loyal to her husband or to her lover, unless she is in a brothel, then she is loyal to her trade. A man is loyal to his friends, his friends to him; if he is not he is a foe, and not a friend. To change the social order you would have to change not only what you are loyal to, but the very meaning of loyalty and friendship. Setting his book in 1925 when the region was in rapid economic expansion, Amado drew a fascinating picture of the accompanying process of social and cultural change.

First of all imagine the plantations, the cocoa trees swaying in the wind, the sea. Men in white linen suits drinking rum and smoking cigars, playing backgammon or roulette, grabbing the behind and breasts of the woman serving as she walks by in the bar. Wives and daughters are at home obediently preparing dishes cooked in palm oil (and if they should get out of hand they are subject to a good horse-whipping). Picture tough guys, without fear of death, preserving their honour with gunplay.

Now see money and cocoa planters and exporters making an overabundance of it. This state of affairs is more or less stable, with no-one fighting for the land anymore, as in the good old days when a man could make his fortune if he was ruthless enough. It is the start of more developed attitudes, of a shift in allegiances. Instead of gaining honour by threats and gunshots, now it is due to the one who promotes his fellow townsfolk by helping to stimulate the town's growth and industry. The old ways eventually succumb to the new as the elite flirt with sophistication: poetry readings and literary societies, dances at the Progress Club — all have their enthusiasts.

Enter Gabriela, who smells of clove and is the colour of cinnamon. She is young, happy and free, laughs loudly and dances as she walks. She loves the simple things in life and possesses an inner state of moral innocence. She is instinctive, primitive, unaware of the expectations and pressures of civil society and mores. Her behaviour is direct and from her heart, like a child's before it adapts to social pressures. Like a child she is uncomplicated, pure and energetic. But she is a *woman*, and the most sexually charged and beautiful the town has ever seen. Her beauty is not just in her physique, it extends through her hands into her food — she is the best of cooks, her seasonings are the source of happiness and bliss. As is revealed when she is hired by Nacib the bar owner to keep house and cook. Immediately, they fall in love. She with his moustache tickling her neck and his great big chest on which she rests her head at night; he with her liveliness and all the ways that it expresses itself.

But what kind of love is this? How can it be understood by the lovers themselves in this *macho* society? How to hold on to this happiness? Nacib grows more jealous by the day and wants to seal their relationship. Perhaps through marriage, but what are the town's expectations for them? Would he have to make a lady of her? Force her into shoes, make her stop dancing, stop laughing, contain her passion? Actually the question is: which of our natural passions is it best to leave alone; laughter, boisterous happiness, sexual enthusiasm and which to tame with institutions and sophistry — killing to preserve one's honour? Is Gabriela's traditional Bahian cuisine better than the grand *Chef de cuisine's* from Rio, with his European accent, his swearwords in French and his sophisticated food and sauces which no one can appreciate? Does it really make sense to sit in a hall and listen to someone talk as you struggle to keep awake, and then is it logical to heap praise on the speaker about his speech, that you neither understood nor cared for? Is it better to sit in the sun, playing with a cat, eating guavas, or to wear shoes that pinch your feet and a fine silk dress that constricts your movements? Beware of the trappings of civilisation, the author seems to be saying.

Amado, much criticised latterly for his gender politics, shows a real concern for the plight of womankind in a macho society, while dwelling too on the femininity of his female characters. What is more, in this book, Amado suggests an alternative to the system that discourages for females what it encourages for men: a certain amount of polygamy. He seems to be saying that love without possessiveness, without the need to control, is the surest way to maintain passion and happiness. AC

She loved many things with all her heart: the morning sun before it got too hot; white sand and the sea; circuses, carnivals, and movies; guavas and pitanga cherries; flowers, animals, cooking, walking through the streets, talking, laughing. Above all, beautiful young men; she loved to lie with them, moaning, kissing, biting, panting and coming back to life. With Mr. Nacib among others. But in this case there was something more. She liked to fall asleep in his arms and dream about the sunshine, the cat, the sand on the beach, the moon in the sky, the food to be cooked. Feeling the weight of Mr. Nacib's leg across her. She loved him very much. Too much. She missed him. She hid behind the door to watch him when he came in at night. He would arrive very late, sometimes drunk. She wanted so much to be with him again, to have him lay his handsome head on her breast...

It was all because she went to bed with Tonico. Why should this be so important, why should it make Mr. Nacib suffer so? It didn't take anything from her, it made her no different, she loved him just the same and couldn't love him more. She doubted if there was another woman in the world who loved a man as much as she loved Mr. Nacib. No matter whether the woman wanted to live with the man or to lie with him, no matter whether she was his wife, his mother, his sister, his daughter, or just his woman, she couldn't possibly love him as much as Gabriela loved Mr. Nacib. All this fuss just because he found her with another man. Dona Arminda said that Mr. Nacib would never take her back. She wanted at least to cook for him. Where would he eat? And the bar — who would prepare the snacks and appetizers? And the restaurant that was about to be opened? She wanted to cook for him at least. 375

## AMADO
Jorge

### Golden Harvest [São Jorge dos Ilhéus]

If you've ever eaten a bar of chocolate then you should read Golden Harvest; it's the extraordinarily potent tale of how cocoa was produced and traded in 1930s Ilhéus in the state of Bahia, Brazil. Like *Captains of the Sand* this is a book from Amado's more politically engaged period of work, and was first published in Portuguese in 1944. It's a splendid, baroque epic of a work, as rich (and as dark) as the finest Parisian *mousse au chocolat*.

Amado's story runs on parallel tracks to reflect the lives of the different social groups that make up the cocoa equation. There are the plantation labourers: desperate migrants from drought-afflicted regions or the luckless descendants of black slaves. They are not merely poor but, deeply indebted to the company store, they are serfs who cannot leave the harsh life of the plantations because of the money they owe the boss. At the other end of the economic scale are the landowners and the up-and-coming cocoa exporters. These latter manipulate prices up and down in a clever scheme to wrest control of the land from the 'colonels', the bold and lawless types who first cleared and planted the terrain. They are a colourful bunch but Amado shows them being swallowed up by the international cocoa traders — a stage in the development of today's corporate global monopolies is rather tellingly illustrated in this book.

In between the poorest and the potentates are a series of characters: prostitutes, poets, pimps and peasants who also ride and fall on the cocoa boom and bust that makes Ilhéus first the 'Queen of the South' and then into a kind of purgatory when all the debts, financial, moral and spiritual, are called in. Amado creates an elemental, a Greek, drama with his Baiano characters who experience the extremes of wealth and poverty, power and impotence...

Read *Golden Harvest* to understand why Amado was Brazil's most revered, most loved author for so many years...RK

If the number of new faces in the streets of Ilhéus had already been large, the boom brought to the cacao zone a multitude from all parts. People looking for work and fortune, adventurers seeking only to exploit the moment. It was during this period that the red-light districts of Aracaju, Bahia, and Recife emptied out, with ships and small sailboats arriving packed with women — white, black, and mulatto, foreign and Brazilian — all thirsting for money, disembarking with huge grins plastered on their faces and drinking champagne at night in the cabaret, where they helped the colonels at the roulette tables. 177

That old epithet of Dr. Rui's (who had died drunk in the middle of the street during Carnival, while making a speech to a group of revellers) had become a classic, used by one and all when referring to the area by the docks where the immigrants put up shanties while waiting to find a work contract: the 'slave market.'

They would ride second-class in the trains to Itapira, Itabuna, Pirangi, and Ácqua Preta, the tenuous hope of a new life on their thin and melancholy faces. In general they went with the idea of retracing their steps a year or two later with money in their pockets, of returning to the land they had left behind and planting it when the rains brought better times. They never returned. They would spend the rest of their lives, scythe on their shoulders and machete at their sides, filling sacks with cacao, pruning fields, drying the beans in sheds and kilns, never getting ahead, always owing the plantation store. Once in a while one would run away, be apprehended and handed over to the authorities in Ilhéus or Itabuna. There was never a single instance of a fugitive being acquitted, despite the agitation stirred up by the communists in some recent cases. They were sentenced to two years in prison, and when they later returned to some other plantation, demoralized and without hope, they had completely given up the idea of flight. There were also a few cases of workers who killed colonels. They were sentenced to thirty years in the Bahia State Penitentiary. 58

## AMADO
Jorge

### Home is the Sailor [A Completa verdade sobre as discutidas aventuras do Comandante Vasco Moscoso de Aragão, Capitão de longo curso]

The portrait of a hero, the famous sailor who travelled the seven seas and has wonderful stories to entertain the bored folk of Periperi, a suburb of Salvador (Bahia), makes up the first part of this novel. And that might have been the only part — a simple account of adventure and bravery — were it not for the envy of the ex-customs inspector Chico Pacheco and the attempt and interest of the narrator in offering us 'the *whole* truth concerning the redoubtable adventures of Captain Vasco Moscoso de Aragão, Master Mariner'.

We get a more realistic account, none the less adventurous or intriguing, though, set in the licentious, friendly and hypocritical society of the port. In the final part, the narrator gives the noted sailor the chance of proving the truth about his own life, and the readers the hints from which to draw their own conclusions. Given both the thesis and the antithesis, as it were, the reader can take on the challenge of finding out the truth or just enjoy this light-hearted combination of adventure novel, love (of all kinds) story and social chronicle of Bahia at the beginning of the 20th century. M-AD

When he reached the top, he stood there, his arms folded across his breast, gazing out at the waters. In that silent pose, his face to the sun, his hair fluttering in the wind (that gentle, perpetual breeze of Periperi), he resembled a soldier standing at attention, or, in view of his impressiveness, the bronze statue of a general. He wore an odd coat, not unlike a military tunic, of heavy blue cloth with a broad collar. Only Zequinha Curvelo, a tireless reader of adventure stories, grasped the fact that there before them, in the flesh, was a sea dog, a man whose element was ships and storms. He whispered his discovery to the others: on the cover of a novel about the sea, the story of a little sailing vessel lashed by tempests on the Sargasso Sea, there was a sailor wearing a coat like that. 10

AMADO
Jorge

## Jubiabá [Jubiabá]

Jubiabá is the story of black Antônio Balduíno, a boxer — with the knack of flattening any white challenger — who gets dressed after bouts in the public urinal in the town square…

Pitched into the world as an orphan, Antônio's life is a fine-grained picture of the life of the Brazilian 'underclass' in the time between the world wars. Growing up in a shanty town perched above the city, as a boy he dreams of conquering a life for himself in the excitement and riches it seems to promise. Highly talented as a song-writer, pugilist and lover his life seems ever on the point of becoming a splendid Hollywood-style success story. Amado makes it clear though that Antônio's blackness (and his poverty) means that things always fall apart and he ends up slaving away on a tobacco plantation, with everything taken from him.

Even those who are emotionally connected to him, his brothers in petty crime, the blond girl of good family, Lindalvina, he adored as a poor black family servant, end up badly and sadly.

At the end of the book Amado tries to persuade us that Antônio achieves redemption on the personal level as a kind godfather to Lindalvina's orphaned child and, politically, as a militant strike leader but this seems like a sentimental (Soviet-style) 'studio ending' to a book that explores lived poverty in a detail that very few great writers have managed. In fact this portrait of poverty and exclusion is a notable achievement. RK

'they…sleep in the sandhills above the docks, looking at the enormous ships, the stars in the sky, and the mysterious green sea'

AMADO
Jorge

## Two Deaths of Quincas Wateryell; A Tall Tale. [A morte e a morte de Quincas Berro d'agua]

When Quincas is found dead one morning lying crumpled in his filthy bed, the woman who found him, found him cold. He had not reached out his hand that morning — as he had done unfailingly every morning since he left his wife some ten years previously — to pinch her behind. He didn't make any advances, or behave in his customary scandalous ways. He must be dead, the woman concluded. However, Quincas Wateryell died with a smile on his face.

Some humour and a touch of magic realism will explain the two deaths of Quincas Wateryell, the 'champion rum-drinker... tattered philosopher of the marketplace... loafer par excellence... the vagabond king of Bahia' that he had become, famed for his goodness to his friends.

Goodness and humour, are precisely what his well-respected, conventional family are lacking when, trying to do all that is necessary to maintain their position in the annals of respectability, they pack him neatly into a box, shaved, combed, with shiny new shoes and a freshly bought white shirt and black suit. They dismiss the possibility of a second, more interesting demise, one that would fit more with the man he had chosen to be since rejecting his family. Holding his death certificate, drawn up that morning by a doctor, signed and sealed, firmly positioned in their hand, they try once and for all to close Quincas' fate with it and bring him back within the clutches of their sinister respectability. Amado though leads his hero instead to a fine and worthy end, fit for ballads and legends, with inspirational last words and appropriate good-byes at dawn some twenty hours later.

Set in the disreputable dockside of Bahia and the shantytown street of Tabuão, *The Two Deaths of Quincas Wateryell* is a pocket masterpiece, long enough to fill one pleasant evening. Amusing and craftily written, at the same time it touchingly strums chords of truth, over a glass of white rum on a hot summer evening, with muffled sounds of voices and laughter, a woman singing, and a guitar. AC

Private Martim and Curió resumed their argument about Wide-Eyed Quitéria. Drink had made Curió more aggressive; he raised his voice in defence of his own interests.

Bangs expostulated: 'Ain't you ashamed, fightin' over his girl right in front of him? He ain't even cold yet and you all come crowdin' around like vultures sniffin' fresh meat.'

'He can decide himself,' Breezy ruled. He was in hopes of being chosen by Quincas to inherit Quitéria, his only possession. After all, hadn't he brought him the prettiest little green bullfrog he had ever caught?

'Humph!' the corpse said.

'You hear? He don't like that kind of talk,' the Negro cried angrily.

'Let's give him a swig, too,' the Private suggested, eager to get into Quincas' good graces.

They opened his mouth and poured in a shot of rum, some of which spilled over his collar and down his shirtfront.

'No wonder. Who ever heard of tryin' to drink lyin' down?'

'Let's set him up so he can see us.' They adjusted Quincas to a siting position in the coffin. His head bobbed from one side to the other, and after the swig of rum, his smile grew broader.

'This here's a fine jacket,' Private Martim said, examining the material.

'There ain't no sense in puttin' brand new clothes on a corpse. When you're dead your dead; you go down under the ground, and that's all there is to it....' 74–75

## AMADO
Jorge

### Shepherds of the Night [Os pastores da noite]

Corporal Martim has got married! And is to seek out honest employment! This astounding news shakes the whole community of lowlifes and prostitutes of the city of Bahia. For Martim is a famous, much-loved heartbreaker and cardsharp... In the first (and best) of three inter-linked stories that make up *Shepherds of the Night* Amado rather cunningly details a skirmish in the long battle of the sexes...

The cunningness lies in its core story of a woman, the serially-abused Marialva, desperate to outsmart and emotionally overpower every man who falls in her path and Martim who has, in a rare moment of sentimental weakness, fallen under her spell. The tension lies in when will the inevitable disenchantment occur and who will pull the plug on the relationship that has (almost) everybody gasping and gaping...

In the second part of *Shepherds of the Night* entitled 'Interlude of the Christening of Felício, Son of Massu and Benedita or Ogun's Compadre' a favourite Amado theme appears in some detail; the Afro-Brazilian religion known as Macumba. This section delivers a fairly heavy dose of Macumba gods, goddesses and priestesses with some commentary too on this religion's relationship with Brazil's more official, Catholic, faith.

In the book's final section 'The Invasion of Cat Wood or The Friends of the people' we shift from sex via religion to 'the social question' and witness a 'land invasion' that eventually forms a shanty town of the poor. There's an interesting, cynical account of Brazilian political and media manipulation as landowners, squatters, opposition and government politicians battle it out for 'hearts and minds'. The same lowlife characters of the earlier sections are involved here too.

One could say that in this piece Amado is guilty of a (well-intentioned) sentimentalisation of Brazil's social underbelly; real-life criminals (or prostitutes for that matter) tend to have a harshness and defensiveness — not surprisingly — that Amado almost never shows. Nevertheless, the first and longest section of the book in particular is very clever, enjoyable writing, and full of understanding of the human heart. RK

Martim arrived at the lunch with Marialva. The Homeric *feijoada* was cooking in two kerosene cans, pounds and pounds of beans, sausage, sun-dried meat, smoked meat, fresh beef and pork, pigtails, pigs' feet, spareribs, bacon. Not to mention the rice, the hams, the tenderloins, the chicken in brown gravy, the fried manioc meal, food enough for an army. 110

Pepe had bought that land for practically nothing years before. Not only Cat Wood Hill but large tracts, whose existence he did not even recall for months on end, though he had a plan to divide them up into lots and develop a residential district there when the city expanded toward the ocean... But in any event, he was not going to tolerate squatters' shacks on his land or the presence of trespassers, especially that pack of vagrants. He would order the shacks razed...

One day buildings would go up there, true. But not those miserable huts. They would be spacious houses with broad verandas, apartment houses designed by famous architects, with all the refinements of good taste and of the most expensive materials. Homes and apartments for wealthy people who could pay the price... As for Cat Wood Hill he had thought of putting that aside for his grandchildren, the boy and girl, Afonso and Katia, he in his first year at law school, she preparing to enter college. Darling children, with leftist inclinations in keeping with their age and the times, pretending to be independent, too, with their cars and their launches at the Yacht Club.

Gardens would be laid out there, women of perfect beauty would walk among the flowers in their bathing suits, tanning their bodies on the beach and in the water, making them more desirable and more agile for nights of love. 243-244

AMADO
Jorge

### Showdown [Tocaia Grande]

Showdown was described as giving 'the underside of (Brazilian) history' by B.J.Chamberlain in his 1990 book on Jorge Amado. It's certainly the underside in the sense of being the totally non-respectable version of the founding of a cocoa town in Southern Bahia. Rather than some cleaned-up, long after the fact, official municipal history that skips the brutal realities of first settlement and cuts to heroic 'founding families', and mayors and state officials with suitably long Portuguese-sounding names, it's the story of the mestizo gunmen, peddlers, rapacious land-grabbers, starveling prostitutes and black hired hands who really cut the first turfs...

Showdown proceeds in a classic racy, populist style that is hard to resist; Amado's storytelling simply washes over your objections — yet another gorgeous fifteen-year-old prostitute in town for the delectation of the cocoa 'baronetcy'? Another fine figure of a half-breed hero 'the Captain', loyal and brave servant of his master 'the Colonel', a landowner who has carved out his cocoa land and fortune with the indispensable help of hired guns (and lawyers). It's the Bahian South as Wild West with less shooting, more whoring and no preacher man, honest sheriff or US Cavalry to spoil the fun. This is Brazil not the Protestant frontier of Hollywood Westerns. Although of course, rather curiously, today a kind of rigid frontier Protestantism — originally a U.S. export — is a major force amongst Brazil's poor, tending to replace both the laissez-faire (and upper-class led) Catholicism and the Afro-Brazilian religion so celebrated by this author.

One of the things that made Amado a Brazilian national treasure in his day was his loving attention to the detail of life in Bahia. An example is the figure of Fadul, peddler and subsequently shopkeeper, the founder of commerce in the town of 'Tocaia Grande' or 'Showdown' (thus named because an important gunfight occurred there). Fadul is a larger-than-life Maronite Christian from the Lebanon, and poignantly described here are the contents of his peddler's pack:

'He dropped the heavy pack, heavier every day, the folding ruler he used as a rattle to announce to rich and poor the presence of commerce and fashion in those boondocks. In the pack he carried silks and calicos, cottons, ladies' boots, buskins, thread, needles, and thimbles, ribbons and lace, soap, mirrors, perfumes, tisanes, coloured prints of saints, and scapulars against fevers.'

If that is a tribute to that long-existing race of men, the despised peddlers, who have lived by carrying the little comforts of the town into the most rural of places, the book in itself is a tribute to the New World experience of settlement and the wider one of homecoming and home-making; 'A citizen's homeland is the place where he sweats, weeps and laughs, where he toils to earn a living and build a place of business and residence.' Fadul is Amado's tribute to the immigrant, to the man who struggles to build something in the wilderness.

Amado loves to unravel the long march of historical and economic progress; a progress he always sees as faulty, corrupt, as in his view of the landowner's son who trains to be a lawyer. The young lawyer's graduation is celebrated by a High Mass with the Bishop, a grand ceremony with the State Governor, a ball at the Club and a late-night session at the best nearby brothel. The hypocrisy of this ensemble is underlined by the words of the new lawyer's proud father; 'Lawyers were nothing but a bunch of hornswagglers, good at putting on airs, useful... precisely in order to legitimise violations of law and justice.' In particular Amado has in mind battles over land-title, falsification of wills and rigging of elections, all 'celebrated' in his various books about the cocoa lands.

Nevertheless he puts on display an element of joyful sensuality, of celebration of the body and of sexuality that he finds especially in Afro-Brazilian culture and that he contrasts with European, Catholic influence. Amidst its floods, fevers and fights, *Showdown* provides a thought-provoking human picture of a frontier town. RK

Initially, in order to know the date of the month and the day of the week, one had to consult the only calendar in Tocaia Grande, hanging beside the door of the dry cacao storehouse. At first glance, a print that was a delight to see: a European winter landscape, mountains white with snow and a big hairy dog with a small cask hanging from his neck, a thing to be admired. Pasted underneath the print hung a small thick pad made of printed pages that told the day and date — the calendar, properly speaking — a New Year's present from Colonel Robustiano de Araújo to old Gerino, a loyal fellow.

The proud owner of such a precious item, Gerino would show off the painting to whores and drovers, repeating information he had heard from the colonel: 'In foreign parts it's cold enough to bust your gut and that barrel is chockfull of cachaça to help anybody who might be in need of it.' You couldn't want a prettier or more educational calendar, even if it was unfaithful and uncertain, because old Gerino would let days and days go by without pulling a leaf off the pad, and when he remembered to do it, following the colonel's recommendation, he would take them off haphazardly: one, two, never more than three, economizing on those letters and numbers that were incomprehensible to nearly all residents and strangers. Life went on permanently behind time, and nobody could guarantee exactly whether it was the end of March or the beginning of April, or if it was Wednesday or Saturday...
143-4

## AMADO
Jorge

### Tent of Miracles [Tenda dos milagres]

Set in the city of Salvador da Bahia, Brazil's black capital, this novel brings together themes explored in Amado's earlier work: the social mobility of blacks in Brazil and the struggle against racial discrimination, and the emergence of Afro-Brazilian religious and musical culture onto the national stage, from a situation of obscurity and police persecution.

It is a split-level novel. We follow the life story of the book's black hero, Pedro Archanjo, from the turn of the century through to his death in the 1940s. Archanjo lives these years to the full. He is a leading figure of Salvador's bohemian dockside life, lover of many women, labour agitator in the 1920s, samba composer, popular scholar of Bahian customs, whose fight against discrimination and injustice reflects the wider struggle of Black Brazilians for equality during the first half of the 20th century. Intercalated between the episodes of Archanjo's epic life are the experiences of a North American university professor, who has written a book about Archanjo, and who is visiting Bahia to take part in the carnival celebration of the local figure at the end of the 1960s. This provides Amado with an opportunity to point up the differences in cultural attitudes between North and South Americans.

Typical of Amado's writing, it is a colourful, atmospheric novel, with an emphasis on action, and a wide array of popular characters. Amado's sympathies are, as ever, with the underdogs, who are seen as the true inheritors and preservers of Bahia's unique African-American culture. The price of mobility into the 'whitened' bourgeoisie seems to be to sacrifice these cultural roots, but if we are to understand the book's message, the situation is less dire now than it was fifty years ago. The struggle of men like Archanjo has not been in vain. DB

From the stonemason/corporal Pedro Archanjo inherited the intelligence and bravery cited in the war bulletins, and from Noca, his gentle features and his stubbornness. Stubbornly she reared her child, saw that he had a home and enough to eat, and put him through school, all without a man's support or help. She would never have anyone else, never again indulged in even a passing affair, although there were no lack of followers who hung around her doorstep coaxing her and making offers. From that hard, meagre life with his mother, the child learned to endure and never to give up, but to keep right on going.

Archanjo often thought of her during the fruitful decade of hard work. She had died still young, when the seeds of yellow fever planted in the manure of the city streets grew and put forth deadly blossoms. It was a good year for yellow fever: the disease reaped an abundant harvest, taking corpses even from the houses of the rich, and Noca de Logunedê was carried off with first batch. Not even Omolú could save her. Noca's strength melted into sores, her youthful grace rotted in the alleys among pools of pus. Whenever Archanjo's strength flagged he would think of his mother, laboring to exhaustion from morning to night, locked in a circle of longing, unyielding in her determination to wear mourning forever and to earn the keep of her child with the strength of her own fragile arms. 219

## AMADO
Jorge

### The Violent Land [Terras do sem-fim]

The 'land' in the title is the tropical forest of Bahia (in North-Eastern Brazil) cleared for cocoa production at around the turn of the century; it was a kind of Very Wild West, with riverboats, gamblers, gunmen and adventurers and adventuresses of every stripe. The whole greedy onslaught on tropical nature was masterminded by gangsterish Cocoa Barons, adept at persuading others to do the gruelling ground-clearing and planting, then stepping in to swipe the resultant crop of 'brown gold'.

This is the *early* Jorge Amado, the social novelist, so he has tales of exploitation to tell strong enough to make you choke on your chocolate bar; but this is also *Jorge Amado-style* social realism so there's plenty of sex and sensuality too; this is Brazil not Soviet Russia. The Bahian cocoa zone was Amado's birthplace and early environment so there's a real wish to convince, a heartfeltness in the writing; the little plantation towns under the moon are made intensely, almost absurdly romantic. There's the lyrical evocation of the rainforest running side by side with the story of how the Cocoa Barons accumulated their fortunes through violence and institutionalized corruption. This Brazil is a land where law and redress under the law belong only to the rich and powerful.

*The Violent Land* is a real chronicle of a period and place, with fascinating layers of social detail about the 'conquest of the cocoa lands' and it's the big, bad, bold story that established Jorge Amado as the best known of Brazil's writers. RK

The forest lay sleeping in its never interrupted sleep. Over it passed the days and the nights. The summer sun shone above it, the winter rains fell upon it. Its trees were centuries old, an unending green overrunning the mountain, invading the plain, lost in the infinite. It was like a sea that had never been explored, locked in its own mystery. It was like a virgin whose flesh had never known the call of passion. Like a virgin, it was lovely, radiant, young, despite those century-old trunks. Mysterious as the body of a woman that has not yet been possessed, it too was now ardently desired. 33

## AMADO
Jorge

### The War of the Saints [O Sumiço da Santa]

The writer amused himself with *The War of the Saints*, as he says in the preface: 'It's been fun to write; if someone else has fun reading it, I'll consider myself satisfied'. It's hard not to enjoy reading this breathless narration of the events which took place — at the height of the military dictatorship in Brazil and of revolutionary fervour around the world — during forty-eight hours sometime in the late 60s or early 70s in Bahia.

The disappearance of the sculpture of Saint Barbara, in transit to an exhibition of sacred art, doesn't provide the reader with a detective story — we know from the beginning who is responsible for the theft — but with entangled stories of love, religion and politics.

In a very relaxed way Jorge Amado writes about the famous Brazilian 'syncretism'; the blending of Roman Catholicism with African religions, about high art and popular art, national politics and local 'arrangements', about deep-rooted prejudices and familiar racial intermingling, blending his fictional characters with real celebrities of Bahian society and real history with a well-written plot that joins together reality, invention and the supernatural. M-A D

The land of Bahia, where fate had led him to live and work, a land where everything is intermixed and commingled, where no one can separate virtue from sin, or distinguish the certain from the absurd, or draw the line between truth and trickery, between reality and dream. In this land of Bahia, saints and enchanted ones make miracles and sorcery, and not even Marxist ethnologists are surprised to see a carving from a Catholic altar turn into a bewitching mulatto woman at the hour of dusk. 23–4

## ANDRADE
Mário de

### Macunaima [Macunaíma]

In July 1928, Mário de Andrade, poet, critic and unofficial artistic leader of his generation, introduced Brazil's reading public to what was to become one of the best known and loved figures in the country's literary, theatrical, and cinematic history—Macunaima: the characterless hero.

For much of the nineteenth century, the elite of newly independent Brazil had been happy to see itself reflected in the heroic and liberal self-image of the Romantic Indian warrior. His aristocratic pride, freedom-loving defiance and fraternal loyalty to the white man gave an mythical aura of legitimacy to the semi-colonial world of the plantation-owners and slaves. But the Abolition of slavery in 1888 and the proclamation of a Republic in the following year signalled the demise of that world. The period from the end of the nineteenth century right through to the accession to power of populist Getulio Vargas in 1930 was one of rapid change. While the coffee export sector was still important, Brazil's society and economy were being transformed with large-scale European immigration, the growth of urban centres like São Paulo and the beginning of industrialization. All this was shifting influence away from the 'coffee oligarchy' and towards the cities. For the new urban classes and the military élite the Indian, black and mestizo peasant seemed to offer only negative models of national identity, rooted in a semi-feudal, rural past and, according to the racial theories of the time, in a biological and psychological degeneracy.

Mário de Andrade's novel was far ahead of its time in the radical way it confronted the new reality, refusing the celebratory, essentialist ideas of cultural identity that the Republic expected of its writers. To those who looked towards the Classical traditions and the industrial technology of Europe as a means of fitting Brazil into the 'universal' history of European civilization, *Macunaima* posed a disturbing challenge. For here was an anti-hero, an enemy of order, a failure of progress, a 'characterless' psychological and cultural chameleon. Indian, black, and white all at once Macunaima is an overgrown child, infuriatingly selfish and irresponsible, lazy and oversexed, disloyal and destructive; yet by the same token, irresistibly subversive, irrepressibly mercurial, capable of defeating or escaping his enemies through his infinite adaptability and magical powers of self-transformation.

At the same time, Andrade's prose 'rhapsody' exposed his middle-class city audience to a dazzlingly rich cultural world that had remained until then virtually invisible in the country's literature. This was the world of popular traditions, celebrations, rituals and religious practices through which Brazil's rural and urban masses gave meaning to their experience of life in the first quarter of the twentieth century.

With Brazil beginning to follow the model of European and North American development, the pre-industrial, non-Western communities in the countryside with their fragile ways of life were faced with a dilemma.

Macunaima can be seen as a dramatic reconstruction of that dilemma, as he proceeds on his fantastic journey from the magical pre-industrial cultural universe of the rainforest to the secularised, mechanical world of capitalist modernity. The hero leaves his Amazonian village for the city of São Paulo, in a quest to recover the sacred talisman left to him by the Empress of the forest. Ironically, though, in the course of confronting and eventually defeating his arch-enemy, the cannibalistic business tycoon Piaimã/Venceslau Pietro Pietra, he adapts so effectively to the commercial, technological culture of the city that his entire identity is undermined, and the betrayal of his origins leads inexorably to his self-destruction. DT

While Macunaíma was going about his business he came across the very tall tree known as Voloman. Sitting on a branch was a bright green pepper shrike with red brows. On catching sight of the hero, it cleared its throat and sang, "Look who's coming down the road! Look who's coming down the road!" Macunaíma looked up intending to thank it and noticed that the tree, Voloman, the Tree of Life, was heavy with fruit. The hero had gone hungry for many hours and his belly balked at the sight of all the oranges and lemons, the sapotes and simatoos, the grapes and grenadillas, pineapples and pomegranates, mangoes and mombins, sweetsop and soursop, all kinds of fruit hanging from its branches.

"Voloman, give me some of your fruit!" begged Macunaíma. The tree refused to give him any. Then Macunaíma shouted this spell, twice over, *"Boiôiô! Boiôiô! Quinzama quizu!"*

All the fruit fell from the tree and the hero stuffed himself till he was gorged. This annoyed Voloman so much that it grabbed the hero by the feet and dragged him far away, to the other side of the Guanabara Bay, to a desert isle which had been inhabited in the olden days by Alamoa, a nymph who came with the Dutch. Macunaima was so tired that he just hung there asleep during the flight. Still asleep, he was landed underneath a very smelly bitter coconut palm at the top of which perched a vulture.

At that very moment this bird felt the need to perform its daily duties and covered the hero with its filthy droppings. 60–61

ANJOS
Cyro dos

### Diary of a Civil Servant [O Amanuense Belmiro]

This unjustly neglected novel takes the form of a diary covering the period from Christmas 1934 to March 1936, the year of its publication. It charts the ups and downs, and eventual disintegration, of a circle of middle-class friends who meet for regular beer-drinking sessions in the city of Belo Horizonte, the state capital of Minas Gerais. The members of the circle — the right-wing Catholic Silviano, the communist revolutionary Redelvim, the feminist Jandira, the young socialite and literato with fascist leanings, Glicério, and the repressed civil-servant/narrator Belmiro who sublimates his emotional frustrations in his writing — could easily be taken as a cross-section of the Modernist intelligentsia that had congregated in the country's major cities since the previous decade. More than that, the atmosphere of superficially held convictions, deluded fantasies, scepticism and passivity surrounding the group comes remarkably close to the embittered critique of the Modernist movement that its leading figure, Mário de Andrade, was to write in the 1940s.

One of the flaws of this generation on which Andrade and Cyro dos Anjos seem to agree was its contradictory relationship to its social origins: for all their modern, urbane sophistication, these characters are all sons and daughters of the decadent oligarchies of the rural interior, the old world of the coffee *fazenda*. They still have a foot in that world, like Redelvim, who retires to his family's plantation to recover from his involvement in a suppressed left-wing revolt, or have brought it with them into the city, like Belmiro, with his superstitious and ignorant spinster sisters and his quaintly adolescent, mythical ideas of love. More serious than this, though, is the group's introspective isolation from the social and political realities about which it endlessly, and idly, speculates; something that becomes even more striking on the occasions when we are allowed to glimpse the violence going on outside. For the historical setting for the novel is the period of left-wing, anti-fascist activity whose brutal repression was the prelude to the so-called 'New State', the populist dictatorship of Getúlio Vargas.

Against this background, the seemingly inconsequential philosophical discussions between the characters about the possibility of conviction and action in the modern age take on a special importance. As the trajectories of more celebrated writers such as Oswald de Andrade, Mário de Andrade and Drummond were to prove, the political struggle of the Vargas regime was the test that finally shattered the fragile literary consensus that had held the Modernist movement together, posing the challenge of how to combine intellectual-artistic integrity with commitment to a cause. All of which makes this novel a fascinating reflection on such a crucial moment in Brazil's modern history from the point of view of its intellectual milieu, as well as an alternative to the kind of writing that tended to dominate the literary scene in those years, that's to say the social realist documentary novels of the Regionalists such as Amado and Lins do Rego. DT

'So, you're still caught up in your soft sordid *petit bourgeois* life?'

My answer was simply to ask him if he had a hundred *mil-reis* to lend me (I really needed them).

Jandira smiled, and Redelvim, who was still bitter, answered: 'Being broke doesn't prove a thing. You are the worst of all bourgeois: you are a bourgeois sympathiser, you have no property to defend.'

I made no reply. Redelvim obstinately refuses to understand me. What good are arguments? I know that, in spite of everything, he is my friend and that he will change his mind, now or later on. Why do they insist on classifying men in categories or according to doctrines? The greatest mistake is to offer only radical routes. Socialism, individualism, this, that, or the other....

It is really unfair to want something definite from us, especially when we have examined ourselves and found nothing.

Redelvim loathes me today, but perhaps tomorrow he will understand. It is not easy for sensitive people to resist the attractions of the current political fancies. The most comfortable solution is to give in, to follow the tide. But will we have proceeded honestly, according to our souls?' 92

# AZEVEDO
Aluizio de

## A Brazilian Tenement [O Cortiço]

Crowded, seamy, noisy and bustling tenement houses cluttered urban Latin America during the final decades of the nineteenth century and were beehives of activity for the European immigrants, skilled and unskilled Brazilian workers, slaves and ex-slaves who poured into the imperial capital and port of Rio de Janeiro. Aluizio de Azevedo, a master of realism in Brazilian literature, captures the pulsating throb of the humid, sultry tropical city, caught in the throes of transition from slavery to free labour as the monarchy that had reigned since Brazil's independence in 1822 faced the onset of a Republic.

The tenement house draws residents from near and far and is a microcosm of working people's daily lives and shared intimacies, the whispered or audible confidences that filter through paper-thin walls or echo the shouts and gossipy hilarity of the washer women who curve their bodies over the tubs in the yard outside. Barely is the sun in the sky before Alexandre, the policeman, arranges his appearance in readiness to order the lives of the citizens of the city during his daily beat. Packing their worn and tattered valises are the Italian immigrants who ply their wares door-to-door in the searing sun or endure the squishing of their soaking socks during torrential rainfall. The flashy, sensuous mulatta Rita Bahiana awakens to the sounds of the dance of the evening before and observes her lover, the *capoeirista* Firmo, in the embrace of the *paraty*, the intoxicating cane whisky that is the companion of the poor in good times and bad.

Rita Bahiana's lover was an unambitious mulatto, of slender, wiry build and agile as a goat. Boastful and impertinent, he enjoyed the reputation of being a clever thief who was enabled to live without steady work so long as windows could be pried open or chickens stolen. Past thirty, he looked like a youth of twenty, with his closely knit frame which appeared to be equipped with springs rather than muscles... Occasionally a fortunate evening with dice or at roulette increased his capital, and then would he enjoy a period of riotous idleness with Rita Bahiana, such as they had spent during the last three months. If not with Rita, then with some other, for he often observed that 'women are not scarce when a fellow's got money to spend.' 82–83

The tenement represents a way-station between the very poor who occupy rudimentary shacks on the city's hillsides and the very wealthy who, like the Portuguese merchant Miranda, his unfaithful wife, Estela, and their daughter who live next door to the tenement, uncaringly flaunt their opulent lifestyle, aiming to please and appease those in the imperial court who might bestow upon the family a coveted nobility title. It is to this lifestyle that the Portuguese owner of the tenement, João Romão, aspires. From modest beginnings, the crafty man has gained the confidence and affections of the slave, Bertoleza, convincing her that he purchased her freedom with her savings from the vegetable stand when, in fact, he has expanded his purchases of land and built the tenement house whilst eyeing and eventually purchasing the profitable quarry that lay behind.

Greed, chicanery, lust, and deception favour those who wish to move up the social ladder, only to find that they share the very fate of the monarchy and the slave-based system upon which it rests. *A Brazilian Tenement* and the varied rivalries and tales of the successes and downfalls of its inhabitants entice the reader down the tortuous alleys and back streets of working class Rio de Janeiro, a riveting read of a city and its people as they come of age. NN

He had but one preoccupation — to accumulate wealth. From his garden he picked for himself and Bertoleza only the poorest vegetables and fruits that nobody would buy. Much as he loved eggs, the many his hens produced were sold, to the last one. Not infrequently their food consisted entirely of the scraps from the plates of customers. This was not economy; it was the manifestation of a disease, a mania to possess, to turn everything into money. 18

# AZEVEDO
Aluizio de

## The Mulatto [O Mulato]

Azevedo was an important writer of Brazil's late nineteenth-century transition from Empire to Republic, an exponent of the Zola-esque 'naturalist' style. This is the story of the struggle of a mixed-race man (or 'mulatto') to make his way in a provincial society dominated by a white elite still looking to Portugal, the colonial Mother Country, as the source of all goodness. Brazil in contrast was seen by this highly conservative sector as an inherently corrupting environment, full of corrupt social and ethnic 'types', particularly people with African or Amerindian roots.

Although strongly influenced by the Portuguese Eça de Queirós and Émile Zola, Azevedo doesn't show Eça's light and sure step as a writer. In compensation though his raw material is both very interesting and very Brazilian. Azevedo is an authentic witness of his times (he lived 1857–1913) and delivers a detailed exploration of mentality and daily life in the formative years of modern Brazil.

There's an awful fascination too in the constant stream of racist ideas and fantasies about Black/mixed-race people that Azevedo puts in the mouths of his white characters. Although these characters live cheek-by-jowl with non-white people it makes no difference to their views, so powerful is the simplistic categorisation of racial thinking. *The Mulatto* must be a useful document for understanding the theories of racial superiority which have been so popular and damaging in the last 100 years, in Brazil and elsewhere.

Like his model Eça de Queirós, Azevedo enjoyed laying into the powerful Catholic clergy of the time and the respectable, narrow-minded provincial merchants and officials who were their greatest admirers. Azevedo's anti-clerical attack encapsulated in the character of Canon Diogo resulted in his having to move out of the town of São Luís, Maranhão, where *The Mulatto* is set; the book did however contribute to the movement for the total abolition of slavery active at that time and which finally ended the scandal of Brazil as the world's last slave state. RK

The canon came to life again.
'A priest?!'

'That's what José, his father wanted.'
'What nonsense!' retorted Diogo, getting brusquely out of the chair.
'There are already too many dark-skinned priests in these parts!'
'But compadre, look here, it's not that...'
'What do you mean, my good man? Imagine — becoming priests! Imagine! And you can see what's happening. Why soon there'll be prelates blacker than our cooking women! You think that's proper? The government should take some serious action in regard to this problem! It should ban nonwhites from certain occupations.'
'But compadre...'
'I say put them in their place!'
And the canon grew heated with indignation. 47–48

## BUARQUE
Chico

### Benjamin [Benjamin]

Buarque, a well-known singer-songwriter in Brazil, writes novels which skillfully blur notions of time, space and morality, in a post-modern world where it is increasingly difficult to distinguish between reality and fantasy. In *Benjamin*, the eponymous protagonist, a middle-aged ex-photographic model, observes life and behaves as if he were always carrying a camera with him. He is forever coming across situations or people who remind him of the past, in a series of incredible coincidences. He sees a young woman in the street, Ariela, and begins a fruitless relationship with her, all because she reminds him of the great love of his life, Castana Beatriz. Benjamin fantasises that she is Ariela's mother, and that he was responsible for her death, and before we know it, the plot and prose have us convinced too. We also meet Aliandro, erstwhile wide-boy and prostitute's son who is now a millionaire and candidate for Congress. As Benjamin's celebrity fades, Aliandro and the man who is grooming him for "stardom", G Gâmbolo, are on the up, in a society that is just as incapable of separating truth from deceit as Benjamin, and as we the readers. The opening sequence of the novel forewarns us of the fate of Benjamin, yet Buarque manages to keep us hooked to the end, and the closing sequence, although very familiar, still takes us by surprise. SD

The execution squad was lined up; the order to fire was forceful and the shots produced a single report. But to Benjamin Zambraia they sounded like a drum roll, and he might even be able to tell the order in which the dozen weapons in front of him had discharged. Even if blind, he would identify each rifle and say from which barrel had come each of the projectiles that now tore into his chest, his neck, his face. Everything would be extinguished with the swiftness of a bullet between the skin and its first vital target (aorta, heart, trachea, medulla), and in that instant Benjamin witnessed what he had expected: his existence was projected from beginning to end, like a motion picture, on the blindfold of his eyes. Faster than a bullet, the film could be projected again on the inside of his eyelids, in reverse, when the succession of events might prove more acceptable. And there would still be a small thread of time for Benjamin to see himself once more here and there in situations that he would prefer to forget, the images ricocheting in the recesses of his skull.

## BUARQUE
Chico

### Turbulence [Estorvo]

This is Chico Buarque's first novel but one sees straightway it's not his first piece of writing — he is of course world famous as a composer and performer of songs of love and protest, with a career reaching back to the years of military dictatorship in Brazil (1964-1985). In *Turbulence* there's the same acute eye at work as in his best songs.

The novel has something of a *bossa nova* rhythm in its strange but satisfying leaps of focus, starting off for example with the world observed through the spy-hole in the narrator's front door. When its protagonist leaves his flat he restlessly drags the reader with him through the streets, buildings and suburbs of an often chaotic, sometimes violent city. The book is an up-to-date picture of Rio de Janeiro where, however confusing the trajectory, it's always possible to recognise the lifestyles and thought-patterns of the last two decades — concrete architecture fighting luxuriant nature, high consumerism, electronic gadgetry and the invasion of violence into public and private life. At the centre of its drama is the social apartheid that Rio de Janeiro epitomises so starkly — the paranoia and tension running between the high-rise condominiums of the rich, with their electric fences and security guards, and the gang warfare and narco-trafficking that govern the lives of their shanty-town 'neighbours'.

The characters are not given names but are nonetheless recognisable figures from Brazil's street corners and gossip columns and, although the 'turbulent' flow of the narration is as discontinuous as a dream, it very effectively captures the reality of contemporary Brazil, alive, disparate, scandalous and surprising. M-AD & RK

She twitches her eyebrows in my direction, then looking down again so her hair falls over her face, absorbed in the photos she is sifting into small heaps. They set out a place for me opposite her, some distance away, and she doesn't look up as she passes me photos where there are no people, only parks, streets, snow, repeated landscapes I dispatch in half a minute. They must be photos from the beginning of her trip, when she was lonely and emotionally drained; though she's studied photography, her framing is uneven, she under- or over-exposed, as if she was in rush to finish the film. In the photos she's piling up out of my reach I imagine her now with a fresh complexion, perhaps she's opening her arms on a bridge, having shown a stranger how to handle the camera. And in the more recent photos she's standing behind the milk jug, I expect there are the friends she keeps making, and the friends of friends, and artists and public figures, and the lights of the boat during the farewell dinner. 10

## CALLADO
Antônio

### Bar Don Juan [Bar Don Juan]

Journalist Antônio Callado's *Bar Don Juan* (1971) is the second of a series of novels charting the fate of the Brazilian Left in the period immediately preceding and following the military coup of 1964. It picks up the story from the end of Callado's *Quarup* [see below], in the wake of the defeat of the Peasant League movement and the generals' violent takeover, which left the trade union movement shattered and the orthodox left's strategy of cumulative mass mobilisation and reformism largely discredited. Out of a split in the Communist Party in 1967 there emerged a new revolutionary perspective of urban and rural guerrilla struggle, particularly associated with Carlos Marighela. Callado's novel is a sympathetic but critical assessment of this movement, which had been all but smashed by the time of writing.

The narrative revolves around a group of activists who meet in a bar in Rio's middle-class, beachside Zona Sul in preparation for an ambitious operation to link up with Cuban and Bolivian forces in the far west of the country. Callado's explanation for the failure of the movement partly concerns its lack of a clear and unified strategy and its amateurish idealism and inexperience, the epithet 'festive left' encapsulating the picture of bourgeois, would-be revolutionaries who have to ask for time off work to make the revolution. Callado doesn't make light of the consequences of their activities, however (one strand of the book follows Laura's struggle to come to terms with her experience of torture, which is also the fate of the bookish young Marxist Paulino, deliberately handed over to the police as a stool-pigeon), and the Brazilians' disastrous spontaneism is contrasted to the patient, stoic discipline of their Spanish American counterparts — the novel includes a thinly disguised portrait of Che Guevara, and an exploration of his mythical, charismatic appeal.

However much of the book is concerned with the disparate and ultimately individualistic set of motives driving the characters' involvement in the guerrilla struggle, each of them working through some personal war of his or her own. Mansinho is the most irresponsible and self-indulgent, insecure and unpredictable, his predilection for violent bank raids being likened to his sexual conquests. Geraldino could be the reincarnation of the ex-priest Nando in *Quarup*, still seeking an ideological substitute for his shattered faith. Murta is a mediocre film-maker with apocalyptic leanings, expressing the most extreme and abstract version of revolutionary utopianism, the dream of the total Brazilian revolution to end all revolutions. Gil is likewise looking for the non-existent 'essence' of his country through the medium of literature, and is forever hesitating between political action and artistic isolation, in his impatience with the failures and shortcomings of the struggle as it is. Among the only 'proletarian' members of the group, Aniceto is a former hired gun from the backlands, still in the grip of superstition, while Joelmir is a peasant and a former army sergeant on the trail of universal love, but dogged by a terrible secret. João is the most sincere and politicised of all, but in his obsession with avenging the torture of Laura even he, too, in the end wants, not so much 'to realise the revolution, but to realise himself in it.

If all this sounds depressing, it's worth emphasising that Callado, although writing this sober critique in the immediate aftermath of the guerrilla movement's defeat, never abandons his own stubborn idealism. A surprise ending, inspired by the survival of the Cuban Revolution, leaves open the possibility of a different destiny for Brazil. DT

Gil marched over to the papers he had arranged in piles.

'You're still bent on revolution, aren't you? All right, then, I've collected all the Brazilian revolutions together for you. What you see here is a monument to wasted intellectual effort. Page after page after page of notes for the great romance of the Brazilian revolution....

I've got everything written down and put it all in order, and I've been waiting all this time for a fuse to light it with — some swashbuckling tale of armed resistance lasting six months and producing four corpses. I rounded out my characters, I anticipated events, I placed you all at your posts, ready for action. I made you all so beautiful and terrible, you wouldn't recognise yourselves. I would have been satisfied with any positive gesture in the way of revolution, anything to give me an excuse to turn the whole pack of you loose in the middle of the story, whatever it turned out to be. The characters are right here in these pages, like dry logs laid for a fire. But none of you gave me so much as a spark. No one had gasoline or matches or a lighter. You can create fiction out of almost anything, but inventing a revolution is something else again....

'But we've got to make the revolution,' Geraldino said.

'Go on and make it, then,' said Gil. 153–55

# CALLADO
Antônio

## Quarup [Quarup]

Antônio Callado's political novel was published in 1967, a period of intense political turmoil within Brazil which culminated in the imposition of severe political and artistic censorship by the military dictatorship the following year. The novel charts the political and personal development of Nando, an idealistic young priest who dreams of re-creating a utopian paradise in the Amazon, inspired by the Jesuit mission settlements of the 16th and 17th centuries. Nando struggles with his vows of celibacy, and his realisation of his growing affection for Francisca is complicated by her engagement to his great friend Levindo, a left-wing political activist.

He journeys to the Xingu region to make contact with its indigenous peoples, but his vision of an idyllic Eden is swiftly destroyed as he is introduced to the reality of their plight. The Indians of the region are peoples on the verge of destruction by disease and faced with increasing encroachment of their land. Nando works to contact tribes in the region and is reunited with Francisca who brings news of Levindo's death at the hands of the police. Nando's love for Francisca is finally consummated and the couple returns to the northeast with Nando having finally abandoned the priesthood. The two lovers immerse themselves in the literacy campaign organised by the Peasant Leagues in Pernambuco and Nando becomes a fully-fledged political activist. After the 1964 coup, which ushers in the military dictatorship, Nando and several of his friends are imprisoned and tortured for their beliefs. In the wake of this political clampdown, Nando enters a bohemian world of fishermen and prostitutes, determined to lead a simpler life based on principles of sexual freedom. This alienates him from some of his former political comrades but Nando surprises many of them when he decides to organise a commemorative dinner in honour of Levindo. The dinner is violently suppressed by the authorities who consider Levindo a 'subversive' and Nando narrowly escapes death, fleeing into the backlands to carry on the struggle for liberty by alternative means.

Callado's multilayered novel is an infectious read which is not afraid to explore important themes such as the dichotomy between the personal and the political, the possibility of sexual liberation, and the difficulties inherent in the search for personal and national identity. Nando's voyage of discovery, which takes him literally to the centre of Brazil, is representative of the dilemmas facing many Brazilians during the 1960s. The author, himself involved in the Catholic left from the 1950s, convincingly portrays the obstacles facing those attempting to press for change within Brazil, either individually or collectively. Nando's decision to engage with the reality of life puts an end to many of his illusions, yet at the conclusion of the novel, having symbolically adopted Levindo's name, he offers the fragile hope of a new beginning for himself and for Brazil. SS

When the glasses were empty but the feast had not begun, Nando spoke:

'We're all gathered here together in a festive spirit to honor the memory of the only Brazilian who has ever died fighting for an idea. Being Brazilian means having a date with cancer. Being Brazilian means waiting patiently for tuberculosis. Being Brazilian means dying in bed. Levindo led a group of farm workers and was ready to die to see that they got their pay. Levindo died a beautiful foreign death, and we are here today to eat Levindo's sacrifice and his courage and drink his rich young Brazilian blood.'

Nando raised his glass and said:

'Levindo'

And the multitude raised cups, glasses, and mugs, their answer reverberating as if the big posters had shouted:

'Levindo! Viva Levindo!' 514–5

# CAMINHA
Adolfo

## Bom-Crioulo: the Black man and the cabin boy [Bom-Crioulo]

To read Adolfo Caminha's *Bom-Crioulo* for the first time is a startling and unforgettable experience. Originally published in 1895, the year of the Oscar Wilde trials in England, it was the first major Latin American literary work to take male homosexuality as its central theme. It was also one of the earliest Brazilian novels to have a black man of full African descent as its main character. Yet what immediately catches the attention is the detached, non-judgmental way in which the author deals with his chosen subject. Instead of Victorian moralisation there is a curious ambiguity in the novel's treatment of issues of race, gender and sexuality, which is remarkably modern. And instead of the usual decadent or effeminate character, we have a gay hero who stands out because of his physical strength, courage and masculinity.

*Bom-Crioulo* tells the story of a triangular erotic relationship between a black sailor in the Brazilian navy, a young white cabin-boy and a middle-aged Portuguese landlady. Although usually attributed to the Naturalist school of Émile Zola, the novel is structured along the lines of a classical tragedy, which lends itself to a more open and reflective interpretation. It is a tale of passionate love, sexual desire, jealousy and revenge which manages to be at once both melodramatic and realistic. *Bom-Crioulo* is anchored in the Western literary tradition, with multiple levels of reference to classical literature, such as Shakespeare's *Othello*, and contemporary European fin-de-siècle culture and politics. At the same time though, it is firmly rooted in late 19th century Brazil. It beautifully conveys the brilliant tropical sunlight and the sights, sounds and smells of Rio de Janeiro before the urban reconstruction of the early 20th century. It also provides an interesting insight into living and working conditions in the Brazilian navy at the time. Caminha, a former naval officer, was noted for his protests against flogging as a form of naval discipline.

Critics have long recognised *Bom-Crioulo* as a major work but have been distinctly embarrassed by its open description of a homosexual relationship. In the mid 1980s, during Mrs Thatcher's administration, the American translation was briefly banned by H.M. Customs. In recent years, however, *Bom-Crioulo* has been translated into the major European languages, and it has been increasingly recognised as one of the most important 19th century Brazilian novels and as a truly great literary work in its own right. RH

The same day he was sent to the Fort. And as soon as the sloop, after a strong shove, pulled away from the dock, the new seaman felt his whole soul vibrate, for the first time, in an extraordinary fashion, as if the delicious coolness of some mysterious fluid had been injected into his hot African blood. Freedom poured in on him, through his eyes, his ears, his nostrils, through every pore, in short, like the very essence of light, sound, smell and of everything intangible. Everything around him: the blue plain of water singing against the sloop's prow, the pure blue of the sky, the distant profile of the mountains, the ships rocking among the islands, the motionless houses of the receding city — even his fellow-seamen, rowing with him in measured compass, as if they were all one single arm — and above all, dear God, above all the wide, luminous expanse of the bay, in one word, the whole landscape, gave him such a strong sense of liberty and life that he really felt like crying, crying openly, frankly, before all the other men, as though he were going crazy. That magnificent sight, that landscape had burned itself into his mind forever; he would never again forget it, never again! The slave, the 'runaway Negro' felt he was a real man, equal to other men, happy to be a man, as big as the world itself, with all the virile strength of his youth. And he felt sorry, he felt very sorry for those who'd stayed behind on the 'plantation', working, working, without any salary, from crack of dawn till... God knows when!' 38

# CÉSAR
Ana Cristina

## Intimate Diary [selections from A teus pés, Luvas de pelica and others]

Ana Cristina César's *Intimate Diary* is a compilation of writings by one of the most outstanding figures of Brazil's 'marginal generation', whose life and career were cut short by suicide in 1983. The publication of *A teus pés* (At your feet) the year before her death marked the appearance of a highly original voice, offering with its teasing humour, its provocative blend of intimate self-concealment and self-exposure, a refreshing countercultural alternative to the prevailing language of those years: whether the chauvinistic propaganda of Brazil's military dictatorship or the militant rhetoric of the orthodox left-wing opposition.

César's playground is the artifice of autobiography, through which the reader is drawn into a compelling, but precariously ambivalent relationship with this elusive 'unknown modern woman.' The tease-within-a-tease of her fake letters and diaries seems to allow us privileged access to the most painfully intimate confidences, the minute, daily dramas of physical sensation, psychological mood and personal relations, only to hold us tantalisingly at arm's length with an ironic disclaimer or a smart rebuff.

*Intimate Diary* demands to be read, and heard, as performance, reminiscent of Laurie Anderson's *Home of the Brave*. Such as when Ana Cristina gets up on stage wearing her sensual kid gloves, and opens her suitcase crammed full of postcard images, the pretext for revealing to her curious, excited audience an endless succession of confessional stories that are made of both private and collective fantasy: 'My friends, this is a suitcase, not a top-hat with rabbits. We have cards enough to last the whole night.'

In this sense, the stuff of Ana Cristina's writing is the ever-shifting, fluid terrain of the sketch, whose language refuses to fix meaning or pronounce truths, but rather illuminates the vortex of modern life from a feminine and erotic perspective, one sensitive to its flux and ambiguity.

The stability of language is here dissolved into an effervescence of clichés, allusions, cross-references and tricks. The word is above all the bearer, as well as the filter, of the myriad of cultural icons that bombard and threaten to depersonalise and absorb the individual in the mass industrial age. So the objects of her intimate poetic universe — 'gadgets to amuse me, bedside TV, recording tapes, postcards, notebooks of various sizes, nail clippers, two Pyrex dishes and a lot more' — share a space with the grander public icons of mass culture — *West Side Story*, the Pope in the shanty-towns of Rio de Janeiro, I-Ching, Vaseline ™, Knorr ™ soup, 50p coins — as well as the array of artists who weld together our individual and collective fantasies: Walt Whitman, Carmen Miranda, Tintoretto and Katherine Mansfield, to name but a few.

Ana Cristina invites us to explore this image-saturated universe through her 'aestheticising gaze', with all the risks that trust and fallibility entail: 'I never know for sure how it will turn out. I play the detective.' With her we may discover that, as she says of the Place des Vosges postcard, 'it's as if you can see and grasp it, or you're completely inside it' — this, for sure, defines the seductively bewildering power of Ana Cristina's *Intimate Diary* and the challenge it poses to us, its readers, to live and die with her, 'on the edge'. DT

I thought up a cheap trick that almost came off. I shall have correspondents in four capitals of the world. They'll think of me intensely and we'll exchange letters and news. When no letter arrives I plan to rip the calendar from the wall, in the session of pain. I'm drawing little snakes which are the offspring of rage — they're little rages which mount the table in a cluster and cover the calendar on the wall, ceaselessly writhing. Those plans and tricks — it was me who invented them on the train. 'Train passing through chaos?' — nonsense. A letter arrives from the capital of Brazil which says: 'Everything. Everything but the truth.' 'The characters wear disguises, capes, face masks; all lie and want to be deceived. They want desperately.' On the contrary, the train was passing through civilised countryside. It was a slow train, a local, that stole into tunnels and in these hours I planned still further, planned to raise a smoke screen and abandon my correspondents one by one. Because I make these journeys propelled by hate. In other words, in search of bliss.

That's why I catch trains a quarter of an hour before they leave. Sweetheart, kleptomaniac sweetheart. You know what lies are for. Sweet kleptomaniac heart. 13

# COELHO
Paulo

## The Alchemist [O Alquimista]

Something like Kahlil Gilbran's *The Prophet* but less mystical in its language, this is a book of 'lessons for living', in the form of a young man's journey from initial poverty and ignorance to the acquiring, after many tests and trials, of a degree of wisdom, experience and contentment. The principal theme is of discovering and staying true to one's *destiny*. It is directed at those determined to break out of an inherited niche in the world and who want somehow to excel and achieve more than the acceptable, mediocre minimum in life.

It is a thoughtful book full of genuinely wise points; for example, that 'every blessing ignored becomes a curse' and that intuition is 'immersion in the universal current of life'. Coelho wants us to understand how to connect to landscapes, real and metaphorical ('one must love the desert, but never trust it completely. Because the desert tests all men; it challenges every step and kills those who become distracted'), and to people ('there was a language in the world that everyone understood... the language of enthusiasm, of things accomplished with love and purpose.').

An authentically inspirational book; if you need inspiration or are setting out on a new tack, *The Alchemist* could be a great support, with its truths and its warnings. RK

They crossed the desert for another two days in silence. The alchemist had become much more cautious, because they were approaching the area where the most violent battles were being waged. As they moved along the boy tried to listen to his heart.

It was not easy to do; in earlier times, his heart had always been ready to tell its story, but lately that wasn't true. There had been times when his heart spent hours telling of its sadness, and at other times it became so emotional over the desert sunrise that the boy had to hide his tears. His heart beat fastest when it spoke to the boy of treasure, and more slowly when the boy stared entranced at the endless horizons of the desert. But his heart was never quiet, even when the boy and the alchemist had fallen into silence.

'Why do we have to listen to our hearts?' the boy asked. when they had made camp that day.

'Because wherever your heart is that is where you'll find your treasure.'

'But my heart is agitated,' the boy said. 'It has its dreams,. it gets emotional. and it's become passionate over a woman of the desert. It asks things of me, and it keeps me from sleeping many nights, when I'm thinking about her.'

'Well, that's good. Your heart is alive. Keep listening to what it has to say.' 134–5

## COELHO
Paulo

## By the River Piedra I Sat Down & Wept
## [Na margem do rio Piedra eu sentei e chorei]

Indeed I wept. A macho book written from the perspective of a woman, all about the feminine, *By the River Piedra I Sat Down & Wept* is another one of Paulo Coelho's tales of the search for wisdom. This time, however, we are not in a desert (as in *The Alchemist*), nor in the Bible (as in *The Fifth Mountain*), but in the French Pyrenees, and learning the wisdom inherent in loving. The 'spiritual path can only be travelled through the daily experience of love', and that is why 'sooner or later, we have to overcome our fears'. Pilar and her nameless lover, her estranged childhood companion, travel the journey together of understanding this. They are fictitious, 'but they represent the many conflicts that beset us in our search for love'.

However relevant and interesting a theme, Paulo Coelho's take on it is to be appreciated only by those who are deeply involved with the occult, and for those who are not too bothered about style when they read. The themes deal, as in his other work, with a process toward understanding. The prose is very elementary and irritating for its repetitiveness.

To some also, it might prove disturbing, for once again, Coelho makes reference to a religious figure, the Virgin Mary, meanwhile re-interpreting Christianity, all the while claiming that all religions are the same. In this book we learn of God's feminine face, that all religions all over the world have a Goddess figure, a Virgin Mary, a Great Mother, though her presence, or importance, may seem to have been forgotten. And it is she who encourages us to love, for loving a partner, and marrying, is the only way of serving God. Though in this story it all seems a little one-sided, the woman's role being reduced only to that, and to following her mate.

There is also some reference made to the Carmelite Order, and a rather brash account is given of Saint Teresa of Avila, a Carmelite nun revered for her writing. Science is ridiculed and the book reads like a burst of enthusiasm for a kind of syncretic religiosity, a charismatic and mystical Christianity.

The book, and its popularity, is perhaps a statement that many believe that prevailing Western ideas and lifestyles leave us seriously out of touch with the means to happy human contact. AC

I don't want a lesson in religion, Padre. I'm in love with a man, and I want to know more about him, understand him, help him. I don't care what everyone else can do or can't.

The padre took a deep breath. He hesitated for a moment and then he said, 'A scientist who studied monkeys on an island in Indonesia was able to teach a certain one to wash bananas in the river before eating them. Cleansed of sand and dirt, the food was more flavourful. The scientist – who did this only because he was studying the learning capacity of monkeys – did not imagine what would eventually happen. So he was surprised to see that the other monkeys on the island began to imitate the first one.

And then, one day, when a certain number of monkeys had learned to wash their bananas, the monkeys on all of the other islands in the archipelago began to do the same thing. What was most surprising, though, was that the other monkeys learned to do so without having had any contact with the island where the experiment had been conducted.'

He stopped. 'Do you understand?'

'No,' I answered.

'There are several similar scientific studies. The most common explanation is that when a certain number of people evolve, the entire human race begins to evolve. We don't know how many people are needed – but we know that's how it works.'

'Like the story of the Immaculate Conception,' I said. 'The vision appeared for the wise men at the Vatican and for the simple farmer.'

'The world itself has a soul, and at a certain moment, that soul acts on everyone and everything at the same time.'

'A feminine soul.'

He laughed, without saying just what he was laughing about.

'By the way, the dogma of the Immaculate Conception was not just a Vatican matter,' he said. 'Eight million people signed a petition to the pope, asking that it be recognised. The signatures came from all over the world.'

'Is that the first step, Padre?'

'What do you mean?'

'The first step toward having Our Lady recognised as the incarnation of the feminine face of God? After all, we already accept the fact that Jesus was the incarnation of His masculine side.'

'And so…?'

How much time must pass before we accept a Holy Trinity that includes a woman? The Trinity of the Holy Spirit, the Mother, and the Son?'146–8

# COELHO
Paulo

## The Fifth Mountain [Quinta montanha]

The book begins with a reference to *The Alchemist* and Coelho repeats the central thesis of his first book, 'When you want something, all the universe conspires in helping you to achieve it'. In a sense, *The Fifth Mountain* is a sequel, for, although the content is different, it shares this philosophical perspective. Like other books that Paulo Coelho has written before, *The Fifth Mountain* is about how to to accept and carry the responsibility of living out one's own life or 'destiny'.

He uses the figure of the Biblical prophet Elijah to illustrate his ideas. Elijah set out the conditions for the coming of the Messiah, and eventually, after he was thoroughly tested was sent up to Heaven in a winged chariot of fire. His mission from God was to restore His worship in the Land of Israel, for the king there had married a foreign princess, Jezebel, who was introducing her own (Phoenician) gods to the people.

Though of interest for its biblical content and the imaginative use of the main story and of other biblical figures like Moses and Jacob, Coelho's philosophical argument sometimes founders on its religiosity, the book actually ending with a prayer. Despite this zealousness and the simplistic prose, *The Fifth Mountain* still delivers a powerful message. Only by confronting what is most important to you, and thereby confronting yourself at your most vulnerable, can you scale the wall of frustrations that keeps you from what you want most, that which gives your life meaning. Only by lighting the fire within and burning can we build.

The book's title refers to Jezebel's Phoenician god, Baal, who is believed to live atop the Fifth Mountain. The worshippers of Baal believe there to be a fire where the gods dwell, but that no-one has climbed for fear of the fire. AC

It was difficult to arrange a meeting with King Ahab, many generations before, with the ascension of King Samuel to the throne, the prophets had gained importance in commerce and in government. They could marry, have children, but they must always be at the Lord's disposal so that rulers would never stray from the correct path. Tradition held that thanks to these 'exalted of God' many battles had been won, and that Israel survived because its rulers, when they did stray from the path of righteousness, always had a prophet to lead them back to the way of the Lord.

Arriving at the palace, he told the King that a drought would assail the region until worship of the Phoenician gods was forsaken.

The sovereign gave little importance to his words, but Jezebel — who was at Ahab's side and listened attentively to what Elijah was saying — began to ask a series of questions about the message. Elijah told her of the vision, of the pain in his head, of the sensation that time had stopped as he listened to the angel. As he described what had happened, he was able to observe closely the princess of whom all were talking; she was one of the most beautiful women he had ever seen, with long, dark hair falling to the waist of a perfectly contoured body. Her green eyes, which shone in her dark face, remained fixed on Elijah's; he was unable to decipher what they meant, nor could he know the impact they were causing.

He left convinced that he had carried out his mission and could go back to his work in the carpentry shop. On his way, he desired Jezebel, with all the ardor of his twenty-three years. And he asked God whether in the future he could find a woman from Lebanon, for they were beautiful with their dark skin and green eyes full of mystery. He worked for the rest of the day and slept peacefully. The next morning he was awakened before dawn by the Levite; Jezebel had convinced the king that the prophets were a menace to the growth and expansion of Isreal. Ahab's soldiers had orders to execute all who refused to abandon the sacred task that God had conferred upon them.

To Elijah alone, however, no right of choice had been given: he was to be killed.

He and the Levite spent two days hidden in the stable south of Gilead while 450 nabi [Hebrew, 'prophets' ed.] were summarily executed. But most of the prophets, who roamed the streets flagellating themselves and preaching the end of the world for its corruption and lack of faith, had accepted conversion to the new religion. 13–14

## COELHO
Paulo

### The Pilgrimage [Diário de um mago]

Written in such a dull and simplistic narrative style — 'After I had driven for an hour or so, I began to feel the fatigue accumulated from the night before' — *The Pilgrimage* needs to convince us rather with its subject matter. In theory this is interesting, compelling even, for those of us who feel we have to engage in 'the inner jihad', the struggle to overcome the lower self and be somebody other than what comes easiest.

But such is the laziness here — 'an old medieval-style house' and 'paintings such as Buñuel's Milky Way' — are particular gems, that one has to work hard to see the gleams of light and wisdom that could be found buried in here, amongst the cheap knock-offs of that great 1970s bore Carlos Castañeda. Coelho does nevertheless touch on a fascinating historical and personal phenomenon: the pilgrimage.

A real book about the inner experience of pilgrimage would be Herman Hesse's brief masterwork *Journey to the East* [Die Morgenlandfahrt] (reviewed in the *Babel Guide to German Fiction*). Coelho though eventually offers some useful ideas about living which justify this book, as long as we don't kid ourselves we're reading literature. There's a useful introduction for example to the triad *eros, philos, agape* — 'for the ancients, enthusiasm meant trance, or ecstasy' — which is a part of the jigsaw to living with enthusiasm that's to say, living. Coelho in fact maybe has too much enthusiasm when he sets out to write — but will we condemn him for that? RK

Normally, we allow enthusiasm to elude us when we are involved in... mundane activities, those that have no importance at all in the overall scale of our existence. We lose our enthusiasm because of all the small and unavoidable defeats we suffer... And since we don't realize enthusiasm is a major strength.. we let it dribble through our fingers...
107

## COELHO
Paulo

### The Valkyries: An Encounter with Angels [Valkírias]

The angels the reader will encounter in the Paulo Coelho version, are Wagnerian to the degree that Wagner would have liked to have come up with them — biker-chicks, riding Harleys and wearing leather kicking up dust in the Californian desert. Their leader, Valhalla, is the keeper of wisdoms such as, how to talk face to face with your personal angel.

In this 'true story' exposé of the author's 'quest for Knowledge' we get a step by step guide, complete with advice on praying, on how to make your soul grow. This is however apparently not another New Age self-help book, but is presented as a true story, an occult tale about a warrior-magus' confrontation with the heart of modern Evil.

To some it may be frightening material; the constant praying, talk of angels, magi, stages of initiation, warriors, and Satanism. But if you enjoyed *The Alchemist*, here it is again, the behind-the-scenes look at the 'spiritual quest' of the author himself. For here apparently we have the context in which his book was written. In the beginning, the author places a copy of the manuscript for *The Alchemist* in the hands of his 'Master' in the 'Tradition', (AC)

'What is this?'

'A way of saying thank you. And of passing on to others all the love you taught me.'

J. opened the package. It contained almost two hundred typed pages, on the first of which was written *The Alchemist'*

Paulo's eyes were gleaming.

'It's a new book', he said. 'Look at the next page.'

There was an inscription written in longhand: 'For J., the alchemist who knows and uses the secrets of the Great Work.'

## CUNHA
Euclides da

### Rebellion in the Backlands [Os Sertões]

Described variously as 'our finest book', 'the great national epic' and 'the Bible of Brazilian nationality', *Rebellion in the Backlands* is an extraordinary, impassioned attempt to explain one of the most traumatic events in Brazil's modern history: the civil war that, between 1893 and 1897, pitted a self-styled rebel community of devout Christians in the Northeastern interior against the massed forces of the Republican state. The refusal of this Canudos settlement to bow to the will of what it considered to be the godless, illegitimate authority of the regional government, its resistance through four successive military campaigns against professional soldiers and modern weaponry, and its final annihilation amidst acts of barbaric cruelty, struck at the heart of the nation's moral sense of self and unity. How, asked Euclides da Cunha, could a country aspiring to stand shoulder to shoulder with the modern, civilised nations of the twentieth century declare a war to the death on its own sons, its most ancient, founding peasant forbears?

Da Cunha, very much a product of the science-obsessed intellectual milieu of the early Republic (declared in 1889), started out with the prevailing perspective of the time, as defended by the most of the press, public and government sources: namely, that this was a legitimate struggle of the progressive, French-style Republic to suppress a reactionary, superstitiously Catholic, Monarchist-inspired revolt of savage, backward peasants under the fanatical thrall of a crazed lay-preacher, Antonio the Counsellor. By the time he published his book, in 1902, however, Da Cunha had witnessed first-hand the final stages of the conflict as a newspaper correspondent, and had seen for himself both the stoic heroism of the rebels, 'titans' superbly adapted to their native terrain, the semi-arid backlands or *sertões*, and the incomprehension and brutality of the Republican forces who, as they stepped off the train at the end of the line, seemed to be entering an alien, foreign land.

This immediate, empirical evidence strained against the ideological framework of Positivist and Social Darwinist orthodoxy with which Da Cunha had approached the war, as the inevitable sweeping aside of a degenerate, mongrel race of primitive throwbacks in the country's march to progress. Unresolved to the very end of the book, that tension exposed dangerous contradictions deep within the psyche of the nation as a whole, whose premature and violent imposition of a 'borrowed' Western model of civilisation had failed to take into account the vital contribution that its oldest and most marginalised cultures — the "bedrock of the nation" — had to offer. It is a tension that also explains the peculiarly hybrid character and style of the book, combining the languages of scientific materialism, ethnography, journalism and political commentary, whose result entirely justifies its unique place within the literary canon, despite its being a work of non-fiction.

*Rebellion in the Backlands* amply repays the dedication it demands of its readers, in this fine, classic translation by Samuel Putnam; from the opening chapter 'The Land', a detailed geographical survey of the region's landscape, through the often dated but always fascinating account of its people's ethnic and social evolution in 'Man', to 'The Rebellion', whose dramatic unfolding leads us relentlessly to Da Cunha's own concluding words of dismay at the 'acts of madness and crimes' committed by nations. DT

Canudos was appropriately enough surrounded by a girdle of mountains. It was a parenthesis, a hiatus. It was a vacuum. It did not exist. Once having crossed that cordon of mountains, no one sinned any more. An astounding miracle was accomplished, and time was turned backward for a number of centuries. As one came down the slopes and caught sight of the enormous bandits' den that was huddled there, he well might imagine that some obscure and bloody drama of the Stone Age was here taking place. The setting was sufficiently suggestive. The actors, on one side and the other, Negroes, caboclos, white and yellow skinned, bore on their countenances the indelible imprint of many races — races which could be united only upon the common plane of their lower and evil instincts. A primitive animality, slowly expunged by civilization, was here being resurrected intact. The knot was being undone at last. In place of the stone hatchet and the harpoon made of bone were the sword and the rifle; but the knife was still there to recall the cutting edge of the ancient flint, and man might flourish it with nothing to fear — not even the judgement of the remote future.

But, nevertheless, for the light of a future day, let this passage stand, even though it be one marked by no brilliance, uncompromising, angry, unedifying by reason of the subject matter, brutal, violent, because it is a cry of protest, somber as the bloodstain that it reflects. 665

# CUNHA
Helena Parente

## Woman between Mirrors [Mulher no espelho]

*Woman between Mirrors* is a work of dialogue/inner dialogue about, primarily, the feminine personality and about challenging and exploring female identity. Helena Parente Cunha is a Brazilian writer from Bahia and this intense, experimental work full of revelatory flashes and irony at the very least helps to show that Bahia is not just the land of dusky beauties that Jorge Amado, the most famous writer on Bahia, popularised in books like *Gabriela, Clove and Cinnamon*. Cunha does, however, use images from Afro-Brazilian myth in *Woman between Mirrors*. Brazil, so caught between different traditions; antique Portugal, avant-garde Europe, US mass culture and African religions, is perhaps a uniquely interesting situation to look at in search of the 20th century personality This is essentially the undertaking of *Woman between Mirrors* and of Clarice Lispector's related if more accessible writing.
R K

*When you were little, you still reacted to things. At least a little. Today you don't react any more. Paralyzed, apathetic, alienated, indifferent.*

I'm patient. Being soft but ready to act. I give consent if I'm given consent, I can be patient about accepting people, including the woman who writes me. When I was little, I still hadn't developed very much patience, and I paid for it more than once. Hence the intense fear and panic I felt, that came from my not being able to adjust to my father's temperament. By giving up the things I want, I can live the life I want. Not a bad way to cut down on walls. At peace with my husband and sons.

*What you call peace is your ability to efface yourself.*

The woman who writes me is continually getting into fights because of her egotism, her vanity. She's always insisted on having her own way, whatever the cost. Little by little I stopped making decisions about things. I want what my husband wants. Being soft but ready to act. So simple. There are the windows of my former house. If my father wouldn't let me stand at the window watching the street and the people going by, often I'd start crying, and get punished for it. If I had spontaneously given up my window, I wouldn't have suffered the fear of punishment or felt so terribly sorry. The windows of my former house are shut up.

# DOURADO
Autran

## Pattern for a Tapestry [O Risco do bordado]

Small town life, in the archetypal imaginary town of 'Duas Pontes' ('Two Bridges') in the archetypal but real state of Minas Gerais. Against the backdrop of the 1930s and 40s in a quiet backwater, stories of burning youthful passions, for love, for knowledge, for a wider world. There are some extraordinary set pieces; 'the brothel', 'the dying man', as well as episodes of the violent frontier period but what sticks in the mind is the strange magic of youthful emotion Dourado captures so well.

At the other end of youthfulness the haunting image of Aunt Margarida, in her late thirties, the story of an unmarried woman forced to renounce her sexuality and live in emotional solitude; a classic case of cramped and painful provincial manners being imposed on the spirit of each new generation.

Even if, more than a quarter century after first publication, Dourado's tone sometimes seems slightly sentimental or picturesque, it's clear the reader is in the safe hands of a skilled and self-confident writer, who brings a suggestive picture of a distinct part of the world to life. RK

Loveless, of uncertain age, in appearance older than her years, her eyes sharp or sometimes vacant, floating in distant mists, she was a milky shadow drifting quietly along the corridors, through the bedrooms, the living-rooms, through life. If she would at least devote herself to church work, become one of those altar mice, those camels on which God crosses the desert, she would have an occupation, someone to devote herself to, someone to whom she could give a placid, carefully hoarded love. But curiously Aunt Margarida struggled against that surrender, that destiny which awaited the maiden ladies of Duas Pontes. She wasn't even religious, did no more than go to church with her mother on Sundays. In church her lips were never seen to move even in prayer: her face was opaque, tranquil, vacant in the gilded half light. As if she were not there. 119

# FELINTO
Marilene

## The Women of Tijucopapo [As Mulheres de Tijucopapo]

Following in the footsteps of North-Eastern Regionalist writers like Graciliano Ramos and Rachel de Queiroz, Marilene Felinto paints an angry and poignant portrait of her homeland. Her heroine Rísia undertakes several journeys: first a painful but therapeutic journey back in time to memories of her childhood in the outskirts of Recife. It was there that she used to observe the dysfunctional families (not least her own) in her community and where she soon became aware of the cruelty of which people are capable and of more general social injustices (the novel is set against the political upheavals of the 1960s). The confessional tone of the narrative helps to make it vivid and moving, as do the details of Rísia's life, the tastes and smells of the North-East, the songs she listened to and the games she used to play.

In the present — the 'now' of the novel — Rísia embarks on a lonely odyssey from the impersonal and inhibiting city of São Paulo through the wide open plains where bandits used to roam, to the mythical village of Tijucopapo where her mother was born and where she hopes to find: her origins and spiritual roots; politically committed companions (not the passive victims she is used to encountering); and the love and affection she has been searching for all her life. Far from identifying with her weak but abusive mother, she dreams of joining forces with warrior women who fight for their rights against the forces of oppression. This is her third journey, from fear and vulnerability to confident empowerment.

The narrative takes the form of a defiant letter from Rísia to her mother, interweaving both fond and bitter memories, longings and grudges, dreams, fears and reality. The character is bitter and traumatised by the events of the past but by writing this document she tries to finally come to terms with them. Her colloquial language is saturated with emotion: returning compulsively to key moments and figures in her life, including insults, repeated phrases and questions and occasionally disintegrating into nonsense rhymes or cries of despair or loss. The sudden changes in tense and the obsessive repetitions are sometimes disorientating but Rísia's journey continues onwards and the voice she always longed for speaks out loud and clear. CW

I am leaving the city where I became a woman but where I arrived a child. It appears that the one survived at the cost of the other and therefore I needed to come away. Now I'd like to compose an aria which will send out music as fine as the strings of a violin. An aria-history of my journey from the road through this forest. Of my travels through the forest. An aria that will be the letter I'll write when I get to Tijucopapo, the land where my mother was born. An aria that covers from my departure to my arrival. I want to compose an aria which will recompose my retreat along the road and from the road to the fields, these fields, where I hope to find the flowers I'll paint with wax crayons on my landscape, in the letter to my mother. I want to compose an aria to recompose my rage and turn it into a gentle beloved little girl. I want to compose an aria of love to echo in the caves of this mountain I am on. 72–73

## FONSECA
Rubem

### High Art [A Grande Arte]

*High Art* is a 'literary detective story' set in Rio with political and historical touches involving rich old Brazilian families and right-wing loonies. The male protagonists take plenty of time out for sexual adventures, usually with prostitutes, while the narrative marches on via murders, intrigues and mysteries. There are some very atmospheric bits and pieces, sandwiched between the detectivery and debauchery, which capture the unique combination of squalor and wealth, power and powerlessness that is Brazil.

Within the frenetic and abbreviated irrealism of the detective story lies some acid social comment; seeing the decor of a designer flat — smoked glass, giant aquarium, built-in wardrobes — the cynical private eye describes it as 'Playtime for parvenus in an underdeveloped country'. RK

Homicide was located in a dilapidated building on Avenida Presidente Vargas. From the window in Raul's office you could see the endless line of cars filling the wide avenue that linked the Zona Norte to downtown. The building's walls were dirty and full of holes. Frayed emergency electrical wiring snaked across the floor. The foyer door had broken hinges and looked about ready to fall off. In the corner, on a piece of newspaper, sat a wooden box of ashes, cigarette butts, and dried spittle. The floor Raul worked on was divided by partitions that formed small cubicles where clerks took depositions from defendants and witnesses. The cops wore cheap, informal sports clothes. 103

## FONSECA
Rubem

### The Lost Manuscript [Vastas emoções e pensamentos imperfeitos]

This fast-paced thriller starts off in Rio de Janeiro at Carnival time but soon the action moves to West and East Berlin, swerving to Paris and then back to the Brazilian interior, following an unnamed film-director narrator on the trail of the lost manuscript of the title and at the same time fleeing the clutches of jewel smugglers. On the way he learns about subjects as diverse as the Carnival costume parades, the political developments leading up to Gorbachev's policy of *perestroika* and the healing properties of precious stones. He also manages to seduce a series of beautiful but sarcastic women and to become obsessed by the Russian Jewish writer Isaac Babel (in a way reminiscent of the narrator of Julian Barnes' *Flaubert's Parrot*) and his mythical long-lost last novel. A German producer offers to fund a film version of Babel's *Red Cavalry*, to be directed by the narrator, giving him the chance to get back into the limelight and recoup the losses incurred after his last project, an adaptation of Euclides da Cunha's *Rebellion in the Backlands*.

Fonseca doesn't allow the reader to pause for breath, either because his hero is trying to avoid dangerous encounters, discussing film-making or literature, or meditating deeply on philosophical questions about the nature of life, art and love. The narrator's life and work are inextricably linked — he pictures shots and sets, invents possible plot lines and imagines dialogues, and describes actions and appearances in metaphors drawn from the movies, dropping the names of eminent actors, directors and screenwriters. The characters, too, confuse reality and art — the carnival queen with his extravagant costume, wanting to become a piece of art; the manipulative televangelist creating a holier-than-thou persona on TV; and the narrator compulsively turning his life into a script, at one point quoting Joseph Conrad on the aim of the novelist: 'My task is to make you hear, to make you feel and above all to make you see; that is all, and is everything'. Fonseca's writing is indeed visually evocative, even in the frequent violent and surreal dream sequences.

The novel is an exhilarating mixture of a satire on contemporary Brazilian society (and its devotion to the media), an account of the research which goes into making a film, and a *film noir*, complete with paranoid pseudo-private eye, fast-talking beauties, villains with sinister henchmen and a large supporting cast of colourful and eccentric characters. CW

When I see a film, I think things like: why did the scriptwriter have the character say such-and-such? When I read a book I also think the same thing: why did the author write that? The guys are professional phrasemakers; they should know what they're doing. And I also pay a lot of attention to people talking on the street corner. The Man in the Raincoat had spoken of roast suckling pig. That must have some relevance. At least it told me I was someplace where roast suckling pig was eaten in celebration. Since I had been drugged during the trip, I couldn't say for certain how long I was in the car, but I don't believe it could have been more than five hours. Traveling five hours, let's say, in a van, which isn't a very fast vehicle, I could still be in the state of Rio, if my kidnappers had taken a lot of twists and turns to throw me off — which wasn't very likely — or I could be somewhere in the states of Minas Gerais, São Paulo or Espírito Santo. 255

# GALVÃO
Patrícia

## Industrial Park [Parque Industrial]

Patrícia Galvão's 1933 'proletarian novel' *Industrial Park* records a crucial moment in working class life in the São Paulo of the early 1930s, and so adjusts the rural bias that has dominated impressions of the fiction of that time. *Industrial Park* also reveals the unique perspective of one of Brazilian Modernism's more fascinating but neglected female figures.

In his useful and informative 'afterword' translator K. David Jackson reminds us that Galvão, or 'Pagu' as she was known, was censured by and expelled from the Communist Party in 1930, for her 'individualism and sensationalist agitation', and was forced to adopt a pseudonym, Mara Lobo, for the book's publication. This novel however demonstrates her 'agitational' commitment to transforming the complex and contradictory reality of class struggle into literature.

It is a very different approach from the socialist 'realism' of Jorge Amado, with its unproblematic narratives of feudal decline and capitalist modernisation. Here rather is the disturbingly chaotic maelstrom of social life — the novel's title in fact was taken from a contemporary advertising billboard, whose triumphant celebration of the new capitalist order of things is the object of her satirical critique.

What we are given, rather than an evolving narrative, is a fragmented series of vignettes, juxtaposing the cynical self-indulgence of São Paulo's rich with the daily struggle for existence of the workers, particularly the women, of the immigrant industrial quarter, Braz, on whom they prey. Alongside the exposure of racism, poverty, the exploitation of the textile factories in both its petty and most brutal forms, and the repression of a young trade union movement, it is perhaps Galvão's particular insight into the sexual lives of her characters which, without sensationalism, voyeurism or sentimentality, manages to dramatise the precariousness of their existence. Sexual vitality and sexual vulnerability, that ambivalence encapsulates the optimism and energy of this new social class, its determination to imagine and snatch glimpses of love and solidarity inside and outside the sordid world of factory and slum, yet its all-too easy victimisation in the brothel or the workhouse for single mothers. The novel ends, not with an easy victory for the socialist ideals which the characters struggle to sustain, but with a chance encounter between two of the novel's fleeting figures who, 'clinging together, victims of the same unawareness, cast on the same shore of capitalist ventures, carry salted popcorn to the same bed'.

The novel's style, which its translator describes as having a 'primitive' rawness of rapid-fire, truncated language descends partly from the 'telegraphic' style Oswald de Andrade had explored in his *Manifestos da Poesia Pau-Brasil* and *Antropofágico* (Pagu participated in the Movimento Antropofágico of the late 1920s and was married to Oswald for a time). Like Galvão's fragmented narrative technique, this corresponded to the movement's commitment to deconstruct or explode the illusory and repressive unity of perspective and narrative which had held together Brazil's pre-Modernist self-image.

This style does succeed in conveying the dynamism of the novel's social milieu and usually accommodates the vigorous blend of colloquial and political language which, in another context, might sound like crude sloganeering. DT

Sampson Street moves full in the direction of the factories. It seems like the worn paving stones are going to break apart.
Coloured slippers drag along still sleepy and unhurried on Monday. Wanting to stay behind. Seizing the last small bit of freedom. The girls tell about the previous evening's dates, squeezing lunches wrapped in brown and green paper.

'I'll only marry a worker!'

'Knock on wood! One poor person is enough. Spend my whole life in this shit!'

'You think the rich date us seriously? Only to fool around.'

'I told Braulio that if it's a fling, I'll tear him apart.'

'There's Pedro!'

'Is he waiting for you? Then I'll get lost!'

The powerful cry of the smokestack envelops the borough. The laggards fly, skirting the factory wall, gritty, long crowned with spikes. They pant like tired dogs so as not to lose the day's pay. A small red slipper without a sole is abandoned in the gutter. A shoeless foot is cut on the slivers of a milk bottle. A dark girl goes hopping and crying to reach the black door.

The last kick at a rag ball.

The whistle ends in a blast. The machines shake in desperation. The street is sad and deserted. Banana peels. The residue of black vapours vanishing. Blood mixed with milk. 8–9

## GAMA
José Basílio da

### The Uruguay (A Historical Romance of South America) [O Uraguay]

Published in 1769, *The Uruguay* is one of several late colonial verse epics on the Indianist theme, and the most admired by the Romantic nationalist writers who took up the subject from the middle of the next century as an expression of Brazil's literary independence. There was much about it to inspire them. It was the first substantial text in Portuguese to voice regret, albeit in the mouths of its Indian characters, for the tragedy of Conquest, in the celebrated lines: 'Ye, sons of Europe, would that ne'er the wind/ And wave had borne you hither! Not in vain/ Nature between ourselves and you hath spread/ The water-wilderness, this vasty deep.' What's more, its main protagonists are heroic warriors fighting a war of liberation, in defence of natural, ancestral land rights, and they are given an unprecedented moral and intellectual stature, arguing their case on an equal footing with their European counterparts. And it has a memorable tragic Indian heroine, Lindóia, who takes her own life after being cruelly separated from her lover Cacambo, adding a sentimental dimension to the ravages of colonialism.

The historical episode that provides the basis for *The Uruguay* is the same as that depicted in Roland Joffe's 1986 movie *The Mission*, the campaign by joint Portuguese and Spanish armies to enforce the 1750 Treaty of Madrid by expelling a cluster of Jesuit mission settlements from lands on Brazil's southernmost frontier, on the river Uruguay. For all the destructive impact of the mission experience overall for Brazil's Indians, it is clear that these were successful, prosperous communities and that the Jesuits enjoyed the unreserved loyalty of their Guarani 'wards'. Da Gama takes the official anti-Jesuit line of his time, though (the Portuguese Government was in the process of expelling the Order from all of its dominions), denouncing the missionaries' cynical manipulation of the 'innocent' Indians in the rational, anti-clerical language of the Enlightenment.

What makes the text especially interesting is its tension between Da Gama's justification of the sovereign right of the Imperial authorities to suppress the rebel missions, and his clear sympathy for the Indians' plight and the natural legitimacy of their cause. Among its most memorable passages are the set-piece debate, in Canto II, between the Guarani envoys and the Portuguese commander about the true meaning of liberty, and the warriors' heroic and ingenious efforts in Cantos III and IV to undermine the European invaders' advances, as if working in a magical alliance with their native land. An intriguing detail concerns the likely influence of Voltaire's *Candide* on Da Gama's epic, for the mission Indian Cacambo appears in both texts, which share a similar anti-clerical, Enlightenment perspective. The English edition (presented together with a facsimile of the original Portuguese manuscript) is a posthumously published nineteenth-century version by Richard F. Burton, the famous translator of the *Arabian Nights*, who was British Consul in Santos between 1865 and 1868. DT

'All men know/ How heaven bestowed these fair broad plains we tread/ Free to our fathers and in freedom we/ From our forbears received as heritage/ And free our children shall from us receive./ We hate, we still refuse to bear the yokes,/ Save that the heavens vouchsafed to reverend hands./ The wingèd shaft shall judge between our feuds/ Within a little while and shall your world/ (If of humanity one trace remain)/ Decide betwixt us twain if we defend/ Thou justice, we our God and fatherland.'/

'In fine 'tis war ye want, war ye shall have,'/ Rejoined our General. 'You may now depart/ For open lies the path.' 63–64

# GUIMARÃES ROSA
João

## The Devil to Pay in the Backlands [Grande sertão: veredas]

## The Jaguar [selections from Primeiras histórias and Estas estórias]

One of the two towering figures of post-War Brazilian fiction (the other being Clarice Lispector), João Guimarães Rosa is best known for his great novel *Grande sertão: veredas* (*The Devil to Pay in the Backlands*) (1956), in which he singlehandedly reinvented the mythical and cultural significance of the *sertão* or backlands — the perennial Other of Brazil's coastal, urban civilisation. In the wake of Euclides da Cunha's *Rebellion in the Backlands* (1902) and the Regionalist fiction of the 1930s, the *sertão* had become synonymous with grinding poverty, cultural and economic backwardness and social exclusion. With *The Devil to Pay in the Backlands* Guimarães Rosa added a metaphysical and psychological dimension to that world, whose inhabitants, the *sertanejos*, now grapple with eternal forces: love, violence, good and evil. The *sertão* has become boundless, coterminous only with the universe itself; as his protagonist Riobaldo says, 'the *sertão* is everywhere... the *sertão* is moving the whole time, you just don't see it.'

Riobaldo, now an old man and a rancher in the valley of the São Francisco river, recites his 'caso', an infinitely extended campside tale, to an anonymous listener who stands both inside and outside the narrative (or inside and outside the *sertão*), for he might be an actual character, the author himself, or us, the readers. It is the story of his life's journey as a *jagunço*, a gunman on the frontiers between northern Minas Gerais and southern Bahia, culminating in his leadership of a band of men and his confrontation with a rival gang leader, Hermogenes. Hermogenes has murdered Riobaldo's predecessor and, in order to destroy him, Riobaldo must make a pact with the Devil, to whom he offers his soul in exchange for successfully crossing the deadly hostile region of Liso do Sussuarão.

As in the story 'The Third Bank of the River' translated in the collection *The Jaguar*, the idea of the 'travessia' or crossing takes on a complex symbolic significance at the heart of the narrative, incorporating a whole set of ethical, metaphysical and even psychoanalytical ramifications. One of the most fascinating of these is Riobaldo's homoerotic attraction to a fellow gunman, Reinaldo, whom he addresses with feminine overtones as Diadorim. Diadorim's transexual ambivalence is resolved only when, in his masculine guise, he dies confronting Hermogenes on his beloved's behalf, a sacrifice that may well be the price exacted by the Devil for his pact. If you're already intrigued by what sound like extraordinary Latin American variations on the mysticism of the chivalresque romances or the myth of Faust, then you're well on the way to being hooked by some of the qualities (another is the daringly experimental language) that have made this one of the most studied and written about works of Brazilian fiction.

But Guimarães Rosa's literary universe wasn't only confined to the epic space of the *sertão*, with its cowhands, ranchers and feuding gunmen. In fact, as is clear from the short stories of *The Jaguar*, a brand-new collection, he was the master of an astonishing variety of narrative situations, registers and voices. These could range from a child's bittersweet discovery of life's beauty and transience, to the schizophrenic, stream-of-consciousness monologue of a half-Indian, convinced he is a blood relation of the wildcats he used to hunt; from a would-be scientist's obsessive and ultimately insane pursuit of his own, elusive mirror-image, to poignant, disturbing and even grotesquely comical dramas of family conflict and disintegration, whether the anonymous folk of the rural interior or the oligarchic dynasties who rule over them. At the heart of all these stories, and of the extraordinary prose-poetry in which they are written, is a fundamental, unifying principle: the frontier, the borderland, the between-place — the 'third bank of the river' — where destinies, relationships, identities and words all exist in an endless state of flux.

Paradoxically, though, as well as symbolising the volatility of life, the 'third bank' also seems to hold out the possibility of a resting-place, a transcendant stillness within the maelstrom of existence. In one of many stories built around the theme of the journey — life's journey of challenge and discovery, the existential journey into solitude, alienation and madness, or the journey towards the mystery of death — a small boy is taken to visit the enormous building-site that was the burgeoning new city of Brasília in the late 1950s. Nearly overwhelmed by this spectacle of inexorable change, which he cannot help associating with the prospect of his mother's death, the boy nevertheless finds consolation in the belief that, like the doll he has mislaid, the things and people we lose do not therefore cease to be, but go on existing in a transcendant eternity, a 'somewhere' in memory or in the imagination:

No, his Little Monkey playmate wasn't lost, in the dark, fathomless deep of the world, not ever. For sure, he'd just be strolling, happening along hereafter, in the other-place, where people and things were always coming and going. The Little Boy smiled at what he'd smiled at, suddenly at one with what he felt: outside the pre-primordial chaos, like the melting apart of a nebula.

Perhaps it is this between-place — 'perpetually posing the possible' — that the protagonist's father is searching for in 'The Third Bank of the River' story of the collection, when he sets himself adrift in a canoe, never to come ashore again: a precarious still-point of equilibrium midway across the current, where real time is suspended, where he is gone but not departed, neither here nor there. Like Guimarães Rosa's *sertão*, it lies at the threshold between mythical and historical time, between an ageless past and the encroaching, turbulent present. It resists the corrosive, dispersive forces of change yet equally refuses to be petrified within the inert, determinate confines of ordinary time and space. But to assume this condition of indeterminacy, of permanent flux, and seek to transcend the volatility of our existence by immersing oneself in it, is both a courageous and a perilous act, as the man's son discovers when he offers to take his place in the boat. For one may be swept away and engulfed altogether or left suspended in a limbo of insanity, like the lost soul in 'The Mirror', drifting between his reflected self-image and an elusive essence, or the half-Indian Bacuriquirepa in 'The Jaguar', who cannot escape his dual identity: both the hunter and the hunted, both the wildcat and its human killer.

Only a special kind of narrative language could meet the challenge of this journey into indeterminacy, into the unceasing race of the river: a prose that constantly overflows into poetry, that wrestles with the task of objectifying human experience while remaining faithful to its irreducible mystery and fluidity, its ambiguities and contradictions. Analogous to its subject-matter, the substance of Guimarães Rosa's fiction is language in a state of flux — and therefore essentially poetic —, strangely archaic, rustic and modern all at once, pushing insistently at the bounds of what is unsayable and meaningful. It is a challenge beautifully represented in the little girl Pixie's endless efforts to tell, and re-tell, the improvised tale of 'The Audacious Mariner', in her playfully uninhibited experimentation with the magic of words. DT

The Aldacious Mariner, he did infirmly go off to discover the other places. He went in a ship, and skulduggery, too. He went on his own. The places were far-off, and the sea. The Aldacious Mariner at first missed his mother, his brothers and sisters, his father. He didn't cry. He did duly have to go. He said: — 'Will you forget me?' His ship, the day came for it to leave. The Aldacious Mariner stood waving his white handkerchief, extrinsically, from inside the ship's going away. The ship went from being near to being far off, but the Aldacious Mariner didn't turn his back on the people, away from them. The people were actually waving white handkerchieves too. In the end, there was no more ship to be seen, there was only the sea that was left. Then one of them thought and said: — 'He's going to discover the places that we're never going to discover...' Then, so then, another person said: — 'He's going to discover the places, then he's never going to come back...' Then yet another one thought and thought, spherically, and said: — 'So, he must be a bit angry with us, deep down, without knowing it...' Then they all cried, ever so much, and went home sadly to have their dinner...

# HATOUM
Milton

## Tree of the Seventh Heaven [Relato de um certo oriente]

*Tree of the Seventh Heaven* bathes the senses in a Tropical rainstorm on a foliage-laden patio as ripe mangoes drop all around us. This is the city of Manaus, made famous (and rich) during the Amazon rubber boom, and rather an exotic locale for the Anglo-Saxon reader, made even more so by its focus on a Brazilian-Lebanese family. This is a family with as many secrets as 'the dark cave in the crown of the jambo tree'. A tree that grows in the secluded patio of the family home and seems to represent a dynasty that is both closed in on itself around the 'shame' of a daughter, Soraya, who cannot speak and another who has had an illegitimate child.

Although the storyline is unsympathetic towards the cramped hypocrisy of 'Old World' religion (both Muslim and Christian in this case) it is nevertheless a romantic and affecting tribute to the life of the Eastern part of the Mediterranean world transplanted to the state of Amazonas, Brazil. The 'real' title of the book *Relato de um certo oriente* which might be literaly translated as 'report or story of a certain Orient' gives us the motive behind the book; an account of the otherworldliness of a transplanted culture.

At the same time it lets us see Manaus as something more complex and interesting than the rubber boom town with the opera house in the middle of nowhere. Hatoum believes that an isolated place like Manaus, far off in the Brazilian interior, embodies another kind of time as well as place. Hatoum's Manaus is as visually, sensually rich as Polish-Jewish writer Bruno Schultz' *Cinnamon Shops* [see *Babel Guide to Jewish Fiction*] if less fantastic. His characters are more recognisably real; the German Gustav Dorner, European witness to Manaus's decline, who haunts the dockside with his Hasselblad camera and takes 'pictures of God and everything else in this city worn down by loneliness and decadence'. Or the figure of the family patriarch, the silk trader, who despite his life-affirming motto—'in this world, paradise can be found on the back of a sorrel, in the pages of a few good books, and between the breasts of a woman'—eventually retreats into pious seclusion with his copy of the Holy Koran.

This is a book that amazed Brazil with its mythically powerful account of seclusion and emotional stasis and it will probably do the same for you. RK

Whenever Soraya joined in collecting fruits and flowers, she did so in her own curious way, sitting for a long time staring at the flesh of the velvet heart that is the jambo fruit, or slowly breathing in the fragrance of the poppies and orchids and other flowers. Later I realised she was trying to use smell and sight to compensate for her lack of speech and hearing. Other times, as on that morning, Soraya contented herself by playing with the rag doll Emilie had made her. I remember the doll's face perfectly, it had jutting black eyes, the cheeks of an angel, and if you looked closely you could see that only the ears and mouth were flat, stitched with red thread, a special artifice of Emilie's. Soraya never let the doll out of her sight; she made poppy garlands for it, offered it pieces of fruit, clutched it in her arms when she clambered astride the sheep, and took it to bed with her in a tight embrace. These were glorious days, days full of discoveries. 9

(Dorner) was forever writing down his impressions of Amazon life. The ethics and behavior of the area's inhabitants and everything about the identity and intimacy among whites, mixed-breed river people, and Indians were among his favorite themes. Included in one of his letters from Cologne were several pages entitled 'Looking and Time in Amazonas.' He maintained that the slow gestures and the lost and unfocused look of people here appeal for silence and constitute ways of resisting time or, better, remaining outside time. He disputed the widespread assumption here in the north that people are alien to everything else, born slow and sad and passive; his arguments were based on his own intensive experience in the region, on 'Humboldt's cosmic pilgrimage,' and also on his reading of philosophers who probed what he called 'the delicate territory of the Other.' The letter was full of quotations and circumlocutions: a generous strategy intended to capture the attention of the recipient, whose only response was doubt and hesitations. 100

## LIMA BARRETO
Afonso Henriques

### The Patriot [Triste fim de Policarpo Quaresma]

Around the time of its publication in 1910, *The Patriot* (the Portuguese title translates as *The Sad End of Policarpo Quaresma*) remained, like its author, pretty much marginalised from the literary mainstream. This is perhaps not surprising, as it is a devastating satire, not only on exagerrated patriotism, but also on the crushing bureaucratic conservatism of the Republican state and its official ideology, Positivism. The novel follows the downfall of a self-educated patriot, from his first, eccentric ventures into public service on behalf of his nation, to his eventual execution for treason.

At first sight it is all too easy to attribute this tragic end to the blinkered, chauvinistic nationalism of which Policarpo is certainly guilty, and which often blinds him to the social and political realities surrounding him. His first patriotic endeavour, based on thirty years of library-bound academic studies, is the highly romantic promotion of indigenous and folkloric traditions as the basis for a new cultural nationalism. After some comic incidents involving a suffocating tribal mask and a disappointing encounter with a black woman who turns out to have forgotten the songs of slavery, this culminates in the humiliating public exposure of his proposal to transform Tupi-Guarani into the official language, and he retreats into the disturbing otherworld of a mental asylum.

However, as becomes increasingly apparent, there is another, far more dangerous madness at work in the outside world, the madness of social conformism, of a kind of mental, as well as political, totalitarianism. For it is not so much the impracticality of Policarpo's ideas that earns him ridicule and rebuke (indeed in many respects they reflect an ultra-orthodox point of view, epitomised in a contemporary manifesto of eulogistic jingoism, Afonso Celso's *Why I Boast of my Country)*, as the fact that his sincerity and public-mindedness, his reformist zeal and initiative constitute a provocation to the inertia and passivity of the bourgeois establishment, and to the hypocritical interests of a reactionary status quo. When, for example, he decides to prove the country's agricultural potential by flouting social decorum and literally getting his hands dirty, yes, his ignorance of farming technology and pest control frustrates his efforts. But far more sinister and threatening is the intimidation and obstruction he meets from the local land barons and administrators for his innocent failure to comply with the rules of petty politics and bureaucracy.

In the third and final part of the novel, Policarpo discovers the true meaning of the Positivist slogan of the Republic: 'Order and Progress' (still found on the Brazilian national flag). Having pledged his support as a loyal citizen-soldier for the military President Floriano Peixoto (a real historical figure known as the 'Iron Marshall') in his suppression of the 1893 Naval Revolt, he is horrified as he becomes both witness and instrument of the regime's barbaric treatment of its own subjects. Arrested and condemned for his legitimate, humane protest, in a terrible, Quixotic moment of revelation he is painfully disabused of all the misconceptions that have guided his life until now; above all, the chimera of the Brazilian 'Terrestrial Paradise', under the benevolent guardianship of an enlightened and civilised State. DT

From the age of eighteen patriotism had been the moving force of his life; for its sake he had committed the folly of studying trivialities. What did rivers matter to him? If they were long what difference did it make? How much happier did it make him to have known the names of his country's heroes? Not a whit. The important thing is that he should have been happy. Had he been? No. He called to mind his Tupí, his folklore and his attempts at farming... Had they left in him any trace of satisfaction? None at all. None at all.

His Tupí had been greeted with general incredulity, laughter, mockery and scorn; it had been the cause of his madness. This was his first disillusionment. And agriculture? Again nothing. The soil was not fertile or easy to cultivate as the books said. A second disillusionment. And when his patriotism turned him into a soldier what did he find? More disillusionment. Where was the meekness of our people? Hadn't he seen them fighting like animals? Hadn't he seen them slaughtering countless prisoners? Yet more disllusionment. His life had been one long disillusionment, or rather a series, a whole chain of disillusionments.

His native country as he wished it to be was a myth, a phantasy conjured up in the silence of his study. In the sense that he had imagined it it simply did not exist, neither physically, morally, intellectually nor politically...206

## LISPECTOR
Clarice

### The Apple in the Dark [A Maçã no escuro]

A man wanders through the deserted backlands in search of a new beginning. He wants to escape from the city, forget the past, start his life from scratch, even to the extent of learning how to see, speak and write anew, because modern society has driven him to the brink of madness and he has committed a crime. The man, Martim, reaches an isolated farm where he is begrudgingly employed by the owner, the frosty, authoritarian Vitória, and where he becomes a source of fascination for her young widowed sister-in-law Ermelinda. A complicated emotional triangle forms between these three as Martim empathises intellectually with Vítoria but desires Ermelinda physically. Each of the characters is restless and dissatisfied with their sense of identity: Martim is plagued by existential anguish, Ermelinda longs for self-validation and security, and Vitória struggles to disguise her fear that she has wasted her life and her femininity by devoting herself to the farm.

The narrative records the trains of thought of each character, delving into their psyche, because there is very little dialogue. Instead they communicate through eye and body language, guesswork and intuition. Through silence, meditation and hard physical labour Martim works to purify his relationship with nature, his fellow beings and God, forging his identity anew. He knows, however, that one day he will have to pay for his crime and that the time he has available for soul-searching in peace is limited. The intimate prose probes and lays bare the characters' fears and confusion, showing how intensely they *feel* the world around them. Like G.H. in the novel which followed *The Apple in the Dark* (*The Passion According to GH*), Martim is forced to question everything about himself that he took for granted, and re-formulate his sense of self.

This was Lispector's fourth novel to be published, and the first to be translated into English, maybe because its setting in the *sertão* (in the drought-ridden North-East of Brazil) seemed to associate it with the social realism and political commitment of the Regionalist literary movement. The sense of exile and disorientation in the text may something to do with the fact that she started drafting it when she was living in England, where her diplomat husband was posted, and finished it in Washington D.C., where she concentrated on her writing and bringing up her young sons to try to ease the homesickness she felt for Brazil. CW

And there he was. What he had meant to do was take some notes, nothing else. And the unsuspected difficulty of it all was that he had had the presumption to try to put into words the blink with which two insects can copulate in flight. But who can tell — he asked himself then in the absolute darkness of the absurd — who can tell if that is not the ultimate expression, the way we describe insects coming to glory in the air. Who can tell whether the high point of that description is only and precisely in the wanting of it... (And so he was saving the value of his intention, the intention he had not known how to transform into action.) Who can tell whether our objective was the fact that we are the process itself? Then the absurdity of that truth enveloped him. And if that is how it is, oh God — the great resignation one must have in order to accept the fact that our greatest beauty escapes us, if we are only the process.
184

# LISPECTOR
Clarice

## An Apprenticeship or The Book of Delights
## [Uma Aprendizagem ou O Livro dos Prazeres]

Philosophy lecturer Ulysses meets primary school teacher Lori and, observing her unhappiness while falling in love with her, decides he will instruct her in the art of self-knowledge, confidence and being true to herself. She has been living according to rules drawn up by others and must abandon the persona she uses in public in order to find peace and freedom from social convention. Instead of writing lists to structure her life and hiding behind a mask of make-up Lori loses her inhibitions and becomes empowered.

Ironically, *this* Ulysses stays put while his beloved makes an odyssey of discovery and *this* Lorelei is not the dangerous siren of German myth but a lonely woman longing for someone to love. The love between the characters draws them ever closer, to a stage where they identify almost completely with one another and she learns not to repress her feelings of desire but to embrace them as part of her identity. Even the language used changes over the course of the novel. From jumbled phrases and streams of consciousness mixed up with staccato sentences and a chapter that is one word long, through dialogue and description, the text becomes balanced and lyrical. On a more cynical note, it could be said that Lori's initial intuitive feminine language is being progressively erased by Ulysses' logically structured male language. He is rather pedantic at times and quite rude to Lori in his guidance of her 'apprenticeship'.

Lispector herself was not completely satisfied with the novel which is, admittedly, unusually upbeat and idealistic for her. Nevertheless the character Lori could be identified with the author, who shared her habit of long walks around the streets of Rio and early morning swims on Leme beach, although Lispector never found a perfect partner as her heroine did. CW

'Living,' she said in the disjointed dialogue that only they followed, 'living is so out of the ordinary that I'm alive only because I was born. I know that anybody can say the same, but the fact is that I'm the one who is saying it.'

'You still haven't become accustomed to living?' Ulysses asked with intense curiosity.

'No.'

'Well that's perfect. You are the right woman for me. Because in my apprenticeship there has been no one to tell me the obvious in such an extraordinary way. The obvious, Lori, is the most difficult truth to discern.' And so the conversation would not become too serious he smiled and added, 'Sherlock Holmes already knew that.' 62

# LISPECTOR
Clarice

## The Besieged City [A Cidade sitiada]

One of Clarice Lispector's early novels but newly translated into English, *The Besieged City* chronicles the life and development of a small town, São Geraldo, and of a young woman, Lucretia Neves; as São Geraldo changes over the years so does she.

Lucretia seems carefree, something of a dreamer. She lives in her hometown with a kind of disgust for it, always wishing to be somewhere else. She satisfies her desire to leave for a more comfortable life by dreaming of a different world. She dreams by day and by night. She dreams of a world where objects are alive, where the external world is one with her rather than against her. She lives inside herself.

She sees only one solution to her predicament: to marry a man who can offer her wealth, jewels — who can offer her a life in a big city with hotels, cafés and theatres. For Lucretia a husband would be a saviour. Mateus Correia, a lawyer, offers her all that she wishes for and marrying him she leaves São Geraldo for the big city.

Now that she has left what she considers to be a backward town and lifestyle, she is still dissatisfied. The *bourgeois* life she has entered is not all that magical and soon tires her. She has to fake her happiness and appreciation. She starts to long for what she was dying to leave: São Geraldo.

*The Besieged City* is a story of the internal struggle of a human being trying to adjust to her predicament. Lucretia is estranged from her own life and never finds what she longs for — does she know what it is she so desires or is she a dreamer with fuzzy dreams? Her only way out is to adapt to wherever she is; in São Geraldo she is a young girl, a dreamer, an idealist, married and in the big city a young bourgeois wife, a materialist. She is a prisoner of her dreams, a prisoner of thought-processes that never allow her to reach peace.

In this novel full of rich imagery, of light, darkness, mirrors, water and Nature, Lispector takes a sceptical look at dreams and desire. She looks at marriage with a critical eye as never seeming to provide what one imagines. She writes about a woman who does not fit in anywhere, always struggling with what she wants and what she has or can have.

Written with irony, it is about a woman incapable of freeing herself from her own ideas, from the desire for a safe and settled lifestyle, but who never takes her life into her own hands. MC-L

But the portrait became increasingly different from the sitter and Lucretia Neves considered it the perfect image. The face on the wall, so swollen and signified, carried the mark of destiny in that dazed expression, while she herself... Perhaps she had fallen into the routine of things and the portrait was the unattainable surface, the higher order of solitude — her own history captured for posterity by the photographer without her even noticing.

# LISPECTOR
Clarice

## Discovering the World [A Descoberta do mundo]
## Near to the Wild Heart [Perto do coração selvagem]

'I am so mysterious that I do not understand myself' CL

Clarice Lispector is universally recognised as being the most original and influential Brazilian woman writer of her time. In feminist circles she is revered as an intensely feminine writer who articulates the needs and concerns of every woman in pursuit of self-awareness. Critics worldwide have found much to admire in her introspective writings, both fictional and non-fictional. Her obsessive questioning of human relationships and the social constraints which threaten rather than foster meaningful communication bring her to the conclusion that the problem of existence is that of language itself.

In 1984, seven years after she died of cancer, Lispector's son edited and published the so-called *crônicas* or columns she had written for the Saturday edition of Rio's leading newspaper, the *Jornal do Brasil*, from August 1967 until December 1973. The book comprises a miscellaneous collection of aphorisms, diary entries, reminiscences, travel notes, interviews, serialised stories, and essays, somewhat loosely defined as 'chronicles': a genre peculiar to Brazil which allows poets and writers to address a wider readership on a vast range of topics and themes. The general tone is one of greater freedom and intimacy than one finds in comparable articles or weekly columns in the European press.

Lispector, the severe and impassioned novelist, confided that she did not find it easy to adapt to the freedom and intimacy of the weekly column. She asked; 'Is the chronicle a story? a conversation? The revelation of one's inner thoughts?' She questioned the wisdom of tackling a genre which to some extent was alien to her introspective nature. Summing up her disquiet, she commented: 'I am apprehensive. Writing too much and too often can contaminate the word', or as Fernando Pessoa once said: 'Speaking is the easiest way of becoming unknown'. Weighing up the contrasting demands of journalism and creative fiction, she shied from the stereotyped role of the garrulous agony aunt and frequently ignored the expectations of her readers with arbitrary forays into other genres. To her surprise, readers reacted positively to her unpredictable contributions and she was soon freely adapting the chronicle to suit her own idiosyncrasies.

The wide range of genres assembled in *Discovering the World* allows the reader to piece together the life and career of this singular personality. The material registers contrasting moods, one moment whimsical, the next grave and questioning, but whatever the topic, the chronicles are disarmingly frank.

Marriage to a fellow-student, Maury Gurgel Valente, — coincided with the publication of her first novel *Near to the Wild Heart*. Lispector was in her early twenties and unknown, but the unusual form and searing effect of this unsparing account of marriage and betrayal attracted the attention of several important literary critics. Sérgio Milliet and Antonio Candido recognized at once that a promising new writer had made her début. Their reviews spoke of a 'sudden break' with established criteria and of a radically different concept of fiction, which opened up new possibilities. Her début was timely.

Marriage to a diplomat meant foreign postings, and for some sixteen years Lispector was to be separated from her beloved Brazil, apart from brief return visits which only intensified her sense of exile and homesickness. She found many of the social obligations required of a diplomat's wife extremely tedious. Writing became increasingly important for her spiritual survival and synonymous with a more meaningful form of existence, and only her work and children kept her sane during those years in alien surroundings. In 1959, she finally separated from her husband and returned to Rio with her children. Despite her Ukrainian Jewish ancestry, Lispector identified completely with Brazil and, most of all, with north-eastern Brazil. Memories of her childhood, especially in Recife, evoked the authentic Brazil where traditions and folklore had been preserved. A slight speech defect made her sound like a foreigner, but she was adamant that she had forged her soul and innermost thoughts with the Portuguese language, 'a difficult language', which she was to transform and even re-invent by means of conceptual refinements, subtle nuances and bold experiments with syntax.

Brazil's other great writer of this century, João Guimarães Rosa, once told her: 'Clarice, I don't read you just for the literature, but in order to learn about life.' Most readers would agree. Her dramatic insights can surprise and shock, amuse and distress. Such is the intensity and vehemence of her prose that it unleashes everything which is gentle and violent in this world of ours. And as she herself confided: 'Everything affects me... I see too much, hear too much, everything demands too much of me.'

The intimate revelations of *Discovering the World* take us through the various stages of womanhood from childhood innocence to awakening perceptions of good and evil. The transition from adolescence to maturity is re-enacted in solemn rites, at once delicate and perilous. The lurking fear of 'ambush', both physical and emotional, is central to many of the narratives. Lispector stalked the uncertainties of life in fear and trepidation, yet anxious and determined to unravel the mystery of existence. She dubbed herself 'an audacious coward' and persisted in confronting life on those terms.

In all her work there is relentless self-questioning. Aware that she was speaking on behalf of all mankind, she was wont to say: 'I am so mysterious that I do not understand myself.' She saw the human condition as flawed, fragmentary and incomplete; the darker side of our nature as being compounded of fear, revulsion, cruelty and hatred. But once having recognised the inherent contradictions, she set about trying to reconcile freedom with restraint, humility with pride, solitude with the need to communicate. Strength had to be drawn from weakness, human reversals transformed into salvation.

The sense of wounded innocence and cruel deception is a constant theme in Lispector's stories and chronicles. She is nevertheless convinced that 'generosity (akin to love) is the very core of our humanity' and that 'wrath and hatred are the sorrow of not being able to love'. For her, 'a world without love is lost', and like most of her women characters she confessed to 'an enormous capacity for love'. Strong convictions, alas, are no guarantee of painless achievement. She understood that love could elevate the spirit but that it could also be deceptive. 'Love', she observed, 'can never be a bad thing. But it often turns out to be hatred in disguise.' Her characters invariably discover that love, whatever its nature, exacts some measure of self-abnegation. As she herself confided: 'I often tire of people. Then it passes and I once more become curious and attentive.' For Lispector, it was most essential that love should never become obtrusive. In one of her chronicles she describes the perfect companion: 'Someone who will not stare too much and cause embarrassment. Someone who will know when to speak and when to be silent, someone who will adore me with discretion and accept both my virtues and faults.'

This might explain why she enjoyed most of all the company of children and her pet animals. Her conversations with young children provide some of the most engaging dialogues in *Discovering the World*. Lispector excels in expressing a child's sense of things. Her maternal instincts were strong and she never tired of observing, guiding, questioning her own sons, but, above all, of listening to them and analysing their responses to the world around them. She insisted: 'One must be gentle, very gentle when dealing with children.' She associated children with spontaneity and a refreshing candour.

The constant presence of some pet animal gave her the same sense of compatibility and mutual understanding. As a child, her family nicknamed her 'The Protector of Animals', and she brought up her own children to love and care for domestic pets. The various species in her narratives and chronicles arouse a wide range of emotions: compassion, fear, amusement and horror, but in general terms she firmly believed that the beasts of the earth enjoy greater freedom and adapt more readily to 'the grace of existence'. She explained: 'An animal never substitutes one thing for another, never sublimates things as we humans are obliged to sublimate them.' Pets offered the loyalty and integrity she often found lacking in human beings.

The haunting fear and mistrust of her own inner nature intrigued Lispector as she struggled to unravel the mysteries of life and death and the ultimate meaning of existence. The nature of God, matter, spirit, and human misery is explored time and time again throughout her work. She asks: 'What is anguish?' then gives her own answer. 'This search of mine for meaning is in itself a kind of anguish. This is something which starts with life, for when they cut the umbilical cord there is pain and separation'. Like the man who came close to suicide in one of her chronicles, we can only survive by finding a register mid-way between pianissimo and fortissimo. The temptation to abdicate was often overwhelming. But in the end, Lispector saw life as a mandate. Death held no fears for her, only its prelude.

Guided by inner rather than external voices, solitude and silence were an essential part of her spiritual armour. She agreed with Thomas Merton that 'true solitude separates a human being from others so that he or she might develop all that is good in their heart and soul'. She astutely observed that 'the solitude of others saves us from solitude, just as self-imposed solitude can save us from being submerged by the excessive love of others'. An habitual insomniac, she learned how to value silence and converse with the night. In her own words: 'There is a great silence inside me. And this silence has been the fount of my words. And from this same silence has come the most precious thing of all, namely, silence itself.'

Solitude and silence were conducive to 'a state of grace' (another of her favourite phrases), which she was careful to differentiate from inspiration or that spiritual state often attributed to saints. The 'state of grace' to which she referred was that enjoyed by ordinary people who suddenly become totally real, because they are ordinary, human and recognisable, 'an experience capable of redeeming the human condition even while emphasising its cruel limitations.' The spiritual world Lispector inhabited, like that of her fiction, was woven from fragments of experience and intuition. Her search for a faceless god was also a search for 'lost essence', a search for unassailable integrity and wholeness.

Fleeting references throughout *Discovering the World* identify the writers at home and abroad who made most impact (she preferred the word impact to influence) on her. Critics have suggested links with Kafka, Joyce, Virginia Woolf, Camus and Faulkner. She herself singled out the names of D.H.Lawrence, whom she described as 'pure fire', and of Hermann Hesse, whose seminal work, *Steppenwolf*, left her spellbound. She defines the book in one of her chronicles as a 'spiritual voyage' and classifies Hesse's novel as a genuine landmark. Lispector clearly interpreted this book as Hesse himself intended: as 'a tale of griefs and needs; still not a book of a man despairing, but of a man believing.'

Her links with the philosophers and writers of the so-called Existentialist Movement have been exhaustively researched and sometimes over-stated. Echoes of Kierkegaard, Heidegger and Sartre can be found in many of her narratives and essays. She shared their anguished awareness of nothingness and encroaching absurdity which renders life intolerable and meaningless. She experienced the same frustration and nausea in the face of life's contradictions and the uncertain nature of human freedom. Endless confrontations with human weakness — her own as well as that of others — when confronted by the enormity of life, led her to conclude: 'We can use our defects as crutches just as easily as our qualities' and continuous errors helped her find new paths.

Inevitably Lispector is compared with Virginia Woolf. Both women were concerned with the inner life of feelings and thoughts and forged a language of their own to describe the fragility of existence and its dark, enigmatic forces. Emotionally they were both prone to alternating moods of elation and depression, of expansiveness and withdrawal. In both writers there are the same intensive perceptions of sound, sight, touch, the same irresistible urge 'to brush, scrape and kindle ...' And most important of all, they shared a belief that plots do not matter, what goes on inside the characters' minds does. Lispector dismissed any direct influence. She claimed only to have read Virginia Woolf's novels some years after the publication of her own first novel *Near to the Wild Heart*.

Lispector's prose, like that of the New Zealand writer Katherine Mansfield whose work she deeply appreciated, appears to flow easily and naturally, governed by feeling and observation rather than by any apparent calculation of its effect. Both built their narratives on fragments of memory and experience with single-minded intensity. Both writers excelled in shorter narrative forms, their eye focused on the moment, the instantaneous, fleeting impressions amidst cross-currents of fear and hope.

Both imposed their own shape on the seemingly intractable realities of life in the shared belief that art is not an attempt on the part of the artist to reconcile existence with his or her vision: it is an attempt to create his or her world within this world.

The enemy of creative lies, she was anxious to enlighten rather than to mystify her readers. Like Mansfield, she was labelled both witch and mystic, but neither of these descriptions does her justice. If she could be stark and pessimistic, she could also be droll and witty. Her sharp eye misses nothing of the human foibles and absurdities around her. The chronicles include amusing encounters with society women, loquacious taxi-drivers, the business-like madam of a brothel, beggars with their own code of honour, unpredictable housemaids who can be formidable and wreak havoc, and an envious nanny whose social ambitions outstrip those of her mistress.

The chronicles also confirm that Lispector was by no means indifferent to political and social problems. The temptation to see her as a tragic muse has misled some critics and readers. The image is not merely false but a travesty of her true nature. Lispector was an astute observer of human concerns. The economic plight and social divisions in her native Brazil were never far from her thoughts. As a child, she had seen the most degrading poverty in the North-eastern provinces, causing her 'to tremble with impotent rage'; in Rio, the starving poor pricked her conscience, and the future of the Brazilian Indians concerned her as deeply as the exploitation of the indigenous population in Portugal's African colonies. She wrote: 'Frankly, I feel socially committed. Everything I write is tied, at least in my mind, to the real world in which we live. Perhaps this aspect of my writing will become stronger one day.' She wrote those words in December 1967, and this social concern had indeed become stronger by the time she came to write her penultimate novel *The Hour of The Star* some ten years later. The plight of her heroine, the ugly, illiterate, impoverished Macabea, who has made her way from Alagoas to the slums of Rio, sums up the Brazilian social drama: the same drama which perplexed and disturbed Lispector as a child in Recife and later influenced her decision to study law in the hope that she might help to reform the country's penal system. When pressed to comment on the question of literature and commitment, she replied: 'It would indeed be strange if I were to remain indifferent to life in my own country. I may not write about social problems but I live them intensely.' Even in her stories for children there is a gentle plea for racial tolerance and social equality. And her mistrust of politicians and their abuse of power is quite unambiguous in two chronicles: 'The Leader's Dream' and 'In Memory of the Man who Stood Down'.

Her political voice may have been understated, her note of censure discreet, but her solidarity on behalf of justice and human dignity was beyond question. She needed no convincing that charity is a futile substitute for social justice and firmly believed that hunger spiritualises no one. Her sentiments echoed those of Carlos Drummond de Andrade, Brazil's most politically committed poet this century, when he declared: 'Time is my concern, time now, men now, life now.'

First and foremost, however, was her commitment to writing. In a television interview, she confessed: 'When I am not writing, I am dead.' She believed that writing could turn a human being into a divinity. And when the words flowed in harmony with thought and feeling, she experienced something akin to ecstasy. She staunchly defended her individual freedom as a writer and insisted: 'If there exists such a thing as expression, then let it emanate from what I am.' Appropriately enough, the last item in this collection leaves us with the question which was to haunt her all her life: 'Could it be that the person who sees most, feels and suffers most?' That was the price she paid for the rare insights she so memorably expressed. GP

# LISPECTOR
Clarice

## Family Ties [Laços de Família]

*Family Ties* is a compilation of thirteen short stories, all linked by one theme: *love*. There is love and how it binds family members together, love and how it imprisons, love and love's cruelty, love and how it liberates or should liberate us.

Writing of love for Lispector is to write about the human condition. Each story is a profound journey into the psychology of her mainly female characters. Strong women, weak women, old women and young girls. Some men too; strong and weak; old and young. All of them seem to be on the verge of experiencing something new; plodding through their daily and often boring routines, set in their habits and habituated to the superficiality that surrounds them. But whether it is a blind man chewing gum, or a dead dog found in the streets, or a buffalo in a zoo, or the smallest woman on Earth in Equatorial Africa, these men and women are all susceptible to experiencing a breaking point in their consciousness.

Lispector brings the external world into the inner reality of each human being she encounters in her writings. And with words that so transparently transmit emotions she relates the intensity of this inner world when questioned, when shattered.

Thus the fifteen year old girl in *Preciousness* who is subjected to the sexual gaze of two young men in the street feels a huge change has occurred, something has been taken from her. The woman of *The Imitation of the Rose* focuses on a bunch of flowers and feels an intensity she has not known before. Should she give away these roses in their unbelievable beauty, or does she want to keep them for herself? The three young men of *Mystery in São Cristóvão*, on their way to a party, stop in a garden to break off a stem of hyacinth, but a white face behind the window stops them, scares them, makes them run away and a great mystery settles on this house.

Writing of love, Clarice Lispector draws us into another's inner self and so draws us into our own inner self. She does it by showing us that love, at the core of the human being and what links us one to the other, however strong it is, very rarely manages to deliver the spiritual liberty we expect of it. And families, as in the story *Happy Birthday,* end up being linked more by superficiality than by love.

In these short stories Clarice Lispector creates worlds that could be ours, worlds and existences that seem totally normal and yet are totally absurd, life that is real and surreal at the same time. She seems to be able write outside the usual social and political constraints with great feeling, wisdom, scepticism and warmth She writes about what is most real and what is kept furthest away from daily life. She questions, she shatters and she (re)creates. MC-L

And she considered the cruel necessity of loving. She considered the malignity of our desire to be happy. She considered the ferocity with which we want to play. And the number of times when we murder for love. She then looked at her mischievous son, as if she was looking at a dangerous stranger. And she was horrified at her own soul, which, more than her body, had engendered that being so apt for life and happiness. And thus she looked at him attentively and with uneasy pride, her child already without two front teeth, his evolution, his evolution under way, his teeth falling out to make room for those which bite best. 92

## LISPECTOR
Clarice

### The Foreign Legion [A Legião estrangeira: contos e crônica]

*The Foreign Legion* is a compilation of short stories and 'chronicles' (a Brazilian literary speciality; short pieces originally published in newspapers, reflections on all and everything, on daily life) from two lines to twenty pages long. They are parcels of thoughts and feelings from Clarice Lispector, as writer, as woman, as human being in society, there are pieces on various subjects — yet all on the same theme: the attempt to reach the essence of life. Whether autobiographical accounts or social commentaries, they embody moments of discovery of a kind of truth, finally or spontaneously attained. There is a connection in this to Sartre's existentialism as embodied in his astonishing *Nausea*. Thus, a 'truth' is discovered: in the darkness of a night 'A Night in February', in the brightness of the day when two people separate 'The Message', in the shape of an egg 'The Egg and the Chicken', in the architecture of a city 'Five Days in Brasilia', in a rainy day 'An Angel's Disquiet', in the acute and unexpected intelligence of a young girl 'The Misfortunes of Sophia' and in the lies we tell others and ourselves 'Without any warning'.

Clarice Lispector's stories are moments in suspension where one sees through the unnecessary and distracting decorations of life. We see beyond the superficiality of the conversations of two people who love each other but cannot communicate 'A Sincere Friendship'. The title of the story 'A Bottom Drawer' is the perfect metaphorical expression of the content of the stories, as well as of the manner in which Clarice Lispector writes. With her writing she gets to the bottom of the drawer. She empties out all its contents and lets it be full of its own emptiness, letting what is at the very bottom come up, in precisely chosen words.

As in her book *Family Ties* Clarice Lispector speaks of love, of the courageous or the cowardly choices we make in life, of honesty towards ourselves, of our never ending search. She takes us on a journey to try to understand ourselves knowing pertinently that it is (almost) impossible — so that we remain a *Foreign Legion* to ourselves and to others, with maybe our only valid hope: to conquer our own freedom. M C-L

Did I understand? No. Nor do I know what I understood at the time. But just as far as one brief moment I had seen with horrified fascination the world is my teacher — and to this day I do not know what I saw — so I understand us, even though I shall never know whom I understood. I shall never know what I understand. Whatever I understood in the park was, with the shock of extreme sweetness, understood by my ignorance. An ignorance which stood there — in the same numbed solitude as the surrounding trees — an ignorance which I fully recovered with its incomprehensible truth. There I stood, the girl who was too knowing by far, and beheld how all that was unworthy in me served both God and man. All that was unworthy about me, was also my treasure. 26–27
But do they understand each other? They have never thought of understanding each other. They have brought themselves as their only banner.' 200

# LISPECTOR
Clarice

## The Hour of the Star [A Hora da estrela]

The great Clarice Lispector's penultimate book, published in the year of her death in early middle age. Her respected translator Giovanni Pontiero said she 'narrates from within'; a way of suggesting her astonishing ability to create intimacy with her readers, not through the gossipy divulgation of real or faked personal trivia, but an intimacy based on mastery of what she is saying combined with *heart*. Heart that is not just that engaging *Brazilian* humanness but, in her tenderness for children, animals, hurt souls there is something of her Ukrainian Jewish background too.

*The Hour of the Star*, the story of poor Macabéa, a girl with no real talents, accomplishments or gifts — except her ability to accept humility and humiliation as if they were entirely natural things — is Clarice's testament for many reasons. Partly because it hits that fundamental question in Brazil and elsewhere: Do you care? Also because in it she succeeds so well with her ideas about writing and her ideas about life, about women's lives, about Brazil. In Macabéa, immortalized in a brilliant film version directed by Suzana Amaral, she has created a character whose life was a kind of opposite to her own — Lispector herself was a successful writer and the beautiful, cosmopolitan wife of a diplomat — and she has used her sympathy and writerly talent in a marvellous piece of observation and creation.

*Hour of the Star* begins with a dialogue with the reader so that when the 'facts of the case' (as Macabéa's life and past is revealed) become known, the trust previously created makes them rebound in the reader's thoughts. Clarice does not write from a great distance but whispers in your ear and Macabea, who is at one extreme of the human condition where 'sadness was a luxury' reaches us as all the more human for that.

Reading the book is not a sad experience as it is often appallingly funny; all Macabéa's conversational tidbits and world-view are supplied by 'Radio Clock', a downmarket FM station that intersperses a constant stream of time announcements with the kind of desperate 'interesting facts' only Radio DJs know. *Hour of the Star* is quite possibly the best Brazilian book ever translated into English, appalling, delightful, accessible but also radical and accomplished. RK

When she realized that her remark about the animals displeased Olímpico, she tried to change the topic of conversation:

'On Radio Clock they used a word that worried me: mimetism.'

Olímpico eyed her disapprovingly:

'That's not a nice word for a virgin to be using. Why do you have to keep on asking questions about things that don't concern you? The brothels in the Mangue are full of women who asked far too many questions.'

'Is the Mangue a district?'

'It's an evil place frequented only by men. This won't sink in, but I'm going to tell you something. A chap can still get a woman on the cheap. You've only cost me a coffee so far. That's your lot. I won't be wasting any more money buying you things. Is that clear.'

Macabéa thought to herself: he's right. I don't deserve anything from him because I've wet my knickers. 55

# LISPECTOR
Clarice

## The Passion According to G.H. [A Paixão segundo G.H.]

*The Passion According to G.H.* is a novel that somehow feels like a series of short stories, for each chapter starts with a sentence that gives it a theme.

The overall theme is the same as in the compilations *The Foreign Legion* and *Family Ties;* getting to the bottom of the drawer, coming to an understanding of oneself and the essence of life, embodied, essentially and symbolically, in the notions of love, honesty, truth.

In *The Passion according to G.H.* a woman is questioned existentially about her life but the questions find no answers. It speaks of the self-discovery of a human being, in this case the almost anonymous G.H., as she questions, criticises and wonders. It examines the processes G.H. goes through to arrive at a greater understanding of what her life is about, of what *life* is about. The crucial moment is the premeditated killing of a cockroach in the door of a wardrobe.

Before this pivotal event, G.H. is the one others see and perceive; she is her name. A name that we only know as G.H., her initials as engraved on her suitcase. Even though she is a questioning being she lives in ignorance of her own self. Something is amiss but it eludes her. She tries to grasp it but only distances the possibility of understanding by talking too much, by delaying the silence that could reveal what she is searching for. She defines herself by all her possible external extensions, never being truly honest — she fears what honesty may reveal.

There is one prerequisite for change: that the deadly safe routine should be broken. Killing the cockroach is more about killing than about what she kills; about what she kills in herself and the effect that has on her life from that moment on. It is about her starting to be truthful with herself and leaving the fears that immobilise behind her, replacing them with a new courage that will set her free, that will give her the necessary space to undergo her mystical experience of the self.

In a story where all seems to fall apart, chapters are symbolically linked by the last sentence of the previous chapter becoming the first sentence of the next one, as if this sentence were a unique point of reference to hold onto, for everything else is being questioned, dismantled, thrown away. The 'I' of the protagonist is fused with the 'I' of the author in a way that allows any reader to fully identify with G.H. and 'become' her.

This is a world where external and internal realities rarely meet, or coincide, but when they meet, an explosion takes place. She tries to bring into her meaningless life of routine the dimension of the spiritual embodied in rituals, here the killing of a cockroach and what follows it; the 'eating' of the cockroach. The 'moment of truth' in itself becomes crucial. In this moment, everything else disappears so that G.H. can make sense of what this killing means to her, of how it changes her. M C-L

But are the discoveries of infancy like those made in a laboratory, where one finds what one will? Was it when, only when I became an adult that I started to fear and grew the third leg? Can I, as an adult, have the childlike courage to love myself? to lose oneself is to go looking with no sense of what to do with what you might find. The two walking feet minus that extra third one that holds a person down. And I want to be held down. I don't know what to do with the horrifying freedom that can destroy me. But while I was held down, was I happy? Or was there — and there was — an uncanny restless something in my happy prison routine? Or was there — and there was — that throbbing something to which I was accustomed that I thought throbbing was the same as being a person? Isn't that it? Yes, that too... that too... 5–6

## LISPECTOR
Clarice

### Soulstorm [*selected stories from* A via crucis do corpo *and* Onde estivestes de noite]

Twenty-nine stories and fragments from Lispector's collections: *The Way of the Cross* (1974) and *Where you were at night* (1974) are gathered together here. They range in style and topic, from abstract streams of consciousness, like 'Silence' or 'A Report on a Thing', quasi-autobiographical reflections like 'The Man who Appeared' or 'For the Time Being' and the surreal nightmare images of 'Where you Were at Night', to complex and disturbing narratives like 'The Body' or 'In Search of Dignity'.

As Lispector reveals in her 'Explanation', the first half of the collection, the stories from *The Way of the Cross*, were commissioned by her editor, who wanted: "three stories which, said he, had really happened. The facts I had, only imagination was missing. And the subject was dangerous." The stories she came up with deal with social misfits and taboo subjects such as bigamy, homosexuality, sexual promiscuity, murder, prostitution, rape, and sexual desire in the elderly. This sounds rather shocking but in fact the stories are so exaggerated and parodic that they seem like tragicomic cartoons! The style is often like that of a tabloid newspaper or a fanciful soap opera, using short dramatic sentences and dialogues.

In trying to portray "reality" and the secret lives of the people she observed around her she created eccentric and colourful characters, admitting that her work could be seen as trash. "But there's a time for everything. There's also a time for trash. This book is a bit sad because I discovered, like a foolish child, that it's a dog's world."

This close observation of people's intimate lives continues in the second half of the book, but the joky tone of many of the earlier stories is lost in favour of melancholy and soul-searching, leading to philosophical musings about love, life and death. CW

Senhora Jorge B. Xavier simply couldn't have said how she had gotten there. Not through some main gate. It seemed to her that, half in a dream, she had entered through a kind of narrow opening in the midst of the rubble of a building under construction, as if she had slipped sideways through a hole made just for her. The fact is, the first she knew, she was already inside.

Yes, the first she knew, she realized that she was very much inside. She was walking endlessly through the subterranean passages of the Maracanã Stadium... 73

# LISPECTOR
Clarice

## The Stream of Life [Água Viva]

This liquid narrative (the title very literally means "living water") is difficult to define in terms of genre, style or theme; as it says, "categories pin me down no longer." It is like a series of pulsations, the narrator's attempts to capture the "now-instant", "it" or "X" of a fleeting moment or sudden sensation before it slips through one's net. It does have a narrator, a painter, who describes the artistic creative process by comparing literature to painting and also to music — linking her writing to improvisational jazz. Whilst describing her movements, her insomnia, the cups of coffee she drinks and cigarettes she smokes, she enumerates her seemingly random thoughts, giving the text a sense of immediacy, as if it is being written *as we read it*.

Without a solid structure the words flow irrepressibly forth in what Hélène Cixous in her helpful foreword describes as being "always a question of beginnings." The reader can start to read at any point because the narrative is circular, an idea emphasised in the text with the images of the spinning wheel, the rushing stream, regression to past lives and the cat which, having given birth, eats the placenta! This absence of sense, the concept of "not-knowing", is celebrated in Lispector's other works, such as *The Passion according to G.H.* and the *crônicas* of *Discovering the World*, and upholds the importance of suspending rational thought to embrace the ambiguity and possible multiple meanings of a word or a phrase. This is why Lispector's language is complicated but compelling: she reveals that its meaning is never definitive but shifts from moment to moment, like running water.

The most abstract and least conventional of Lispector's novels, *The Stream of Life* paved the way for her later works *The Hour of the Star* and *A Breath of Life* which are also concerned with the process of writing literature. CW

I don't know what I'm writing about: I'm obscure even to myself. Initially I had only a lunar, lucid vision, and then I clasped that instant to myself before it died and perpetually dies. I transmit to you not a message of ideas but rather an instinctive voluptuousness of what is hidden in nature and that I sense. And this is a feast of words. I write in signs that are more gesture than voice. All this is what I used to paint, probing into the intimate nature of things. But now the time has come to stop painting in order for me to remake myself, I remake myself in these lines. I have a voice. Just as when I throw myself into the outline of my sketch, this is an exercise in life without planning. The world has no visible order, and I have only the order of my breathing. I let myself happen. 16

LUFT
Lya

## Island of the Dead [O Quarto Fechado]

Lya Luft is from Brazil's extreme South, the city of Porto Alegre in the state of Rio Grande do Sul, a zone of Northern European immigration, famous for its German colonies. Luft's writing seems to reflect the teutonic element and all her characters are enveloped by a gloomy northern fog of nameless unhappiness.

However, *Island of the Dead,* despite the gloom, is a concise minor masterpiece. The title refers to a copy of the famous painting 'Island of the Dead' by Arnold Böcklin which comes to dominate the thoughts of the main character, Renata. She is a woman who has arrived at a savage vision of marriage — she followed the emotional impulse to marry and have children but her marriage has turned into passionate hatred for her husband and herself. She has also emotionally rejected her children. Renata is a woman who has absolutely made the wrong move in marrying, violating her own nature, which is artistic and solitary.

This is a fascinating and fairly unusual theme and Luft has the courage as a writer to confront it unsparingly. Apart from the relationship of man and woman in marriage there is an exploration of other intimacies; that of brother and sister in a pair of twins who try to absorb each other absolutely; thereby experiencing a kind of ideal closeness, but it is an intimacy, a union of twin souls that is bought at the expense of everything else. Outside their symbiotic emotional affinity no real contact with any other reality is possible for them.

Overhanging the various kinds of failed relationships is a variety of 'deaths' that these failures of love have engendered; the husband Martin is emotionally dead, Clara, an elder daughter, is sexually dead, poisoned by a perverse liaison at the awakening of her sexuality, the twins are socially dead, another daughter Ella is mentally dead after an accident and one of the twins Camilo becomes actually dead.

Luft says here 'all human relationships involve suffering'; an unfortunate truth everyone has to face sooner or later; Luft's book is a brilliant, valid exploration of how and why that is true, in its way very life-affirming, warning us to steer towards achievable goals in our lives, rather than (ultimately poisonous) over-idealisations of *love*. RK

She had lived with him, slept with him, for many years and had made him suffer. With him she had gone from ecstasy to alienation, from passion to hatred, and with him she had seen disintegrate what they had built to last forever. But an interior gulf had never been overcome. Ardour and sweetness had turned to impatience, after being lovers they had become strangers. Whose fault was it?

A successful pianist, Renata had come down from the concert stage to Martin's world, a matter-of-fact world of strength and rationality. But old enough to have her habits already ingrained. she hadn't been able to change. She had tried to substitute her domestic life for her art, but very soon found her new surroundings vulgar. Until then she had concentrated on herself, she could not share herself with another. With so many demands on her now, she felt impotent.

No, love had not been enough. They had gone through all the stages of a slow, painful separation. They rarely saw each other; actually they avoided each other, fearing new scenes.

Years ago she had said, "I'm nor the type to get married," seeing women her age surrounded by children. After marriage, too late, she realized that she had been right. Even though it could be lonely, difficult, and sterile, her art was less complex for her than human love. 7

# LUFT
Lya

## The Red House [Exílio]

We don't entirely discover where the Red House is but it certainly isn't in that stereotypical Brazil of sinuous mulattas, coffee beans and carnival. Here instead are the themes and images of contemporary European fiction and yet — not exactly.

This is a book about the tides of affectionate connection in women's lives and simultaneously it is about the damage caused by the lack or the destruction of those connections. To an extent there's the caring narrative presence, maternal in a way, one recognises from Clarice Lispector's work. Lya Luft, though, is more sombre, more obsessional and gets at emotional truth in a different way. In *The Red House* she examines the states of mind of a daughter abandoned by her mother. The narrative is driven by the desire of this woman from a disrupted family for stability and fixity in her own adult life. The strength of her need, unsurprisingly, destroys the possibility of achieving it.

Lya Luft has worked a great deal as a literary translator and translated Virginia Woolf amongst others. There is some Woolf in this book — the attempt to go below the surface by looking very hard at the surface of things. So while the days of the nameless 'abandoned daughter' pass in apparently prosaic, cloistered circumstances, we gradually absorb the psychic picture of an individual's feelings and patterns.

Luft writes very well; 'People from the provinces who spoke in whispers and wore a permanent expression of alarm', and although the book is the troubling account of a troubled individual, in a place suffused with that South American, 'Deep South' gloom that never lifts, many readers will find it finally therapeutic and connecting. RK

'It is already evening when I return from work. I shut myself away in my room; the same hovering disquiet as I sit there anxiously waiting. Waiting for whom? Whom am I expecting?

Today it finally dawned on me. This was the hour when Lucas came home from school. Notwithstanding the long hours I had to spend at work, Lucas's existence had been the compass which quietly governed mine: the time he left for school, the time he arrived home, the time for his bath and his meals. Despite my busy life and demanding job, I constantly had to reassure myself: Lucas is all right, he is in good hands and perfectly safe.

Without him I was like a deserted house, doors wide open, the floorboards eaten away once the rats moved in.

My heart tells me: Lucas should be home now.' 98–99

# MACHADO DE ASSIS
Joaquim Maria

## Counselor Ayres' Memorial [Memorial de Aires]

The last of Machado de Assis's novels, published in 1908, the year of his death, *Counselor Ayres' Memorial* has been regarded as his swan-song and, given its melancholic tone, his 'reconciliation with life'. In fact it is much more interesting than that. Its central character is Counselor Ayres, a Brazilian diplomat who has retired to Rio de Janeiro after many years abroad. The novel purports to be his diary for the period between January 1888 and August 1889: in fact, it soon becomes plain to the reader that it also tells a story, centred on an old married, and childless couple, Aguiar and Dona Carmo, and two young people, now in their twenties, the widow Fidélia and Tristão, in whom they have taken an intense interest. Fidélia's marriage was happy, but brief: she also braved the anger of her father, the plantation owner Baron of Santa Pia, to marry the son of a traditional enemy of his. Her husband died in Lisbon, and she has gone into permanent mourning, swearing never to marry again; in the two years since his death, she has visited his grave daily. Tristão is the son of friends of Aguiar and Dona Carmo, and was virtually adopted by them as a child; later, rather than go into his father's business, he decides to get a lawyer's degree and finally to go to Europe with his parents.

The plot has three centres of interest: the first is the wooing and eventual winning of the widow by Tristão, and their emigration to Portugal; the second the story of Ayres's observation of these events; and third, the important political events of 1888 and 1889, principally the end of slavery on 13 May 1888, and the collapse of the coffee economy of the valley of the Paraíba do Sul as a consequence, or as part of this process. In the end, all three of these strands are interwoven, and the novel only takes on its full meaning when that is understood. We should also suspect that not all is what it seems to be: readers of his other novels will be aware that political events are more than just convenient dates for Machado, and that narrators are often unreliable, not only in that they put their own interpretation on events, but because they fail to see hidden truths. JG

Fidelia arrives from Paraiba do Sul on the 15th or 16th. It seems the freed slaves are going to be unhappy. When they learned that she was disposing of the plantation they asked her not to, not to sell it, or to take them all with her. There you are, that is what it is to be beautiful and to have the gift of enslaving! In this kind of enslavement there are no emancipation papers nor laws to free you; the bonds are eternal and divine. It would be funny to see her arrive at the Corte with her freedmen behind her... and for what? And how sustain them? It was hard for her to make the poor things understand that they will have to work for wages and here there would be no means of employing them right away. She promised not to forget them, and, in case she did not come back to the country, to put in a good word for them with the new owner of the property. 82

## MACHADO DE ASSIS
Joaquim Maria

### The Devil's Church [A Igreja do diabo]

Were it not for the strange unease the reader will feel and find hard to identify, these short stories could be taken as pure entertainment; the amazing results of an attempt by the Devil to establish his own church; the useful and profitable findings of a sage in an exotic place; the disappointment and frustration of a man who claims to have come back from the dead; various incidents and accidents in affairs of the heart, updated versions of ancient fables and brief biographies of curious characters.

When, however, the reader starts to appreciate all the richness of details, which are never merely details but convey the meaning of many things which cannot be presented in such short, concise texts; when the uncomfortable complicity created by the narrator with the reader is detected; when the ironical veil is lifted and the sharp critique is revealed, then there are some fascinating meditations on ethics, society and human behaviour.

At the end of the 19th century Machado provides us with a witty depiction of Brazilian bourgeois values and behaviour; but a deeper reading makes us reflect on the relativity of values and virtues, the vanity of knowledge, the doubtful motivation of philanthropy and the emptiness of rhetoric.

Machado's writing career brought him from the lower social classes to the heights of intellectual eminence but he never lost the acute awareness of a society based on exploitation and hypocrisy. The pleasure of reading him is in appreciating his mastery of style and continually finding fresh layers of meaning. M-AD

He proclaimed that the accepted virtues ought to be replaced by others which were the natural, legitimate ones. Vanity, lust and sloth were reinstated, as was avarice, which he declared was only the mother of economy, the difference between the two being that the mother was robust and the daughter skin and bones. Anger had its best justification in the existence of Homer — without Achilles' fury there would have been no *Iliad*: 'Muse, sing the wrath of Achilles, son of Peleus...' 39

# MACHADO DE ASSIS
Joaquim Maria

## Dom Casmurro [Dom Casmurro]

*Dom Casmurro* vies with *Epitaph of a Small Winner* for the title of Machado's most famous novel and is at the top of school and university reading lists in Brazil, though perhaps not for the right reasons. On the surface, it's a sort of *Bildungsroman*, ('novel of achieving maturity') a personal account of the narrator's coming of age in mid-nineteenth century Rio de Janeiro, a time when the Monarchy, the landowning élite and slavery seemed most unassailable. Bentinho ('little Bento'), the cosseted successor to the family fortune, seems to epitomize this stifling world of privileged security, as well as its darker underbelly of vulnerabilities and suspicions.

Before his birth, Bentinho's mother made a pact with God: if He gave her a son, she would bring him up to be a priest. Bentinho has other ideas: he's in love with his next-door neighbour and childhood playmate Capitu Pádua. Too young to assert their own will or to elope, the two children hatch a long-term plan to secure their future happiness. They succeed, but then the adult Bento's growing certainty that he has been the victim of an inexplicable infidelity robs them of everything they've fought for, including the shared joy of raising their own son together. The novel is Bento's account of this betrayal, reconstituted out of affectionate reminiscences and bitterly ironic insinuations in the twilight solitude of his life.

What, though, if our lawyer-narrator has abused his position in order to construct an incontrovertible case for the prosecution? What if his narrative is the meticulously elaborated character assassination of an upstart wife, more intelligent than her husband, intended to rationalise his irrational insecurities and suspicions and restore some meaning to the life that he himself has wrecked? Once we accept that possibility, that we may have become the willing accomplices to some ingenious manipulation, then this wistful recollection is dramatically turned on its head. We are faced instead with the disturbing portrait of infantile paranoia, class resentments and snobbery, and projected guilt, all based on Bentinho's preference for the world of his imagination rather than that of an unsettling reality. His own thoughts and desires are revealed to him like epiphanies: he realises he's in love with Capitu only when he overhears an adult insinuating it; he runs next door and finds her absent-mindedly scratching his name on her garden wall, and they face each other in astonished silence, struck by a realisation that's jumped out at them, taken them by surprise.

A character in Thomas Pynchon's *The Crying of Lot 49* — describes miracles as collisions between cosmic pool-balls, the intrusion of another universe into our own. In *Dom Casmurro* this idea is raised into the principle of Bento's entire existence, except that the miracle is too great for his ego to bear. One such moment occurs when Bentinho, obsessed by Capitu, sees the body of a neglected friend, a poor young neighbour who has died of leprosy. Bentinho's cosily amorous thoughts are annoyingly disturbed by this inconvenient reminder of a less privileged world — as he puts it, people's individual consciousnesses are like separate galaxies, one 'poking its nose' into another from time to time. T M & D T

Of the furniture only the sofa seemed to have understood our situation, offering its services with such insistence that we accepted and sat down. My own particular opinion concerning sofas dates from that moment. They unite intimacy with decorum, revealing the whole house without us having to leave the drawing-room. Two men sitting on one can discuss the destiny of an empire, and two women the cut of a frock; but only by some aberration of nature will a man and a woman talk about anything other than themselves. That was what we did, Capitu and I.
129-30

## MACHADO DE ASSIS
Joaquim Maria

### Epitaph of a Small Winner [Memórias póstumas de Brás Cubas]

Brás Cubas, the 'small winner' whose epitaph this novel writes, is an unremarkable man. A well-to-do citizen of Rio de Janeiro, he tries his hand at politics, journalism and romance, conducting a long and much talked-about affair with an acquaintance's wife. What is remarkable about the novel is its style. After a long illness in 1879 Machado, who had till then been tentatively exploring the relations between Brazil's different social groups, but within the constraints of Romantic convention, turned to a more subjective, psychological form, the model for which he found in Lawrence Sterne's *Tristram Shandy*.

Like *Tristram Shandy*, *Epitaph of a Small Winner* advances not in a straight line but in fits and starts, loops and cutbacks. There is even a 'chapter which I shall not write,' a trick taken directly from Sterne. Where *Epitaph of a Small Winner* differs from *Tristram Shandy*, though, is in the status of its narrator. Bras Cubas, as he writes, is dead, and his autobiography begins not with his conception but with his demise and burial. This unusual set-up gives the narrative a limitlessness that Machado's later novel *Dom Casmurro*, also its main character's

autobiography, lacks. Brás Cubas takes a ride on a hippopotamus to the beginning of the ages and speaks to Nature or Pandora herself, standing beyond all the boundaries of the world he writes about. This limitlessness allows him a cynical relativism, thinly disguised as honest sincerity. within which he can accommodate every cruelty, every hypocrisy with chilling bonhomie. All-encompassing religious or philosophical systems that justify a brutally competitive status quo are mercilessly parodied in Cubas' grim sophistry, a variation on Pangloss' 'all's for the best in the best of all possible worlds'. At the end of life's sordid game he has neither gained nor lost anything much (though, as a good child of the slave owning élite, he has been spared the humiliation of working for a living), so he decides that as he hasn't transmitted his legacy of misery to any descendants, he's come out a 'small winner'.
TM & DT

How glorious to throw away your cloak, to dump your spangles in a ditch, to unfold yourself, to strip off all your paint and ornaments, to confess plainly what you were and what you failed to be! For, after all, you have no neighbours, no friends, no enemies, no acquaintances, no strangers, no audience at all. The sharp and judicial eye of public opinion loses its power as soon as we enter the territory of death. I do not deny that it sometimes glances this way and examines and judges us, but we dead folk are not concerned about its judgement. You who still live, believe me, there is nothing in the world so monstrously vast as our indifference. 75

## MACHADO DE ASSIS
Joaquim Maria

### Philosopher or Dog? [Quincas Borba]

This novel is one of Machado de Assis' greatest, as important as *Posthumous Memoirs of Brás Cubas* or *Dom Casmurro* — it was published in 1891, midway between the two of them. Its central character is Rubião, a poor schoolmaster who inherits a very large sum, and a dog, from the mad philosopher, Quincas Borba, who appears in the *Posthumous Memoirs*, and is the author of a philosophy, 'Humanitism', a demented mixture of positivism and Darwinism: its main contention is that the world (including the transatlantic slave trade) exists for his own personal benefit. Not surprisingly, when Rubião inherits, he sees the point, and decides to move to Rio de Janeiro, then the capital of Brazil and by far its most important city, to enjoy his wealth. On his way, he encounters an 'interesting couple', Cristiano Palha (literally, Christian Straw) and his wife Sofia. They help him set up house in Rio: in the process, Rubião lends money to Palha, and falls for his wife. In a beautifully observed triangular relationship, in which she is the lure who always leads Rubião on, but never actually gives way to him, they gradually fleece him.

Around these central figures are a number of important minor characters: the failed, or rapidly failing politician Camacho, who inveigles Rubião into giving him money to set up a newspaper to promulgate his views, a brilliant parody of pomposity and belief in the sound of words; Rubião's hangers-on, Freitas and Carlos Maria, the latter a study in intense narcissism, who flirts with Sofia (with her collaboration) and finally marries an innocent girl from a plantation, Maria Benedita, who admires him as much as he does himself. Palha and Sofia are a study in social climbing — he through money, she through her contacts with 'society' women like Dona Fernanda, the wife of the plodding politician Teófilo — she herself is an object-lesson in how virtue produces its own rewards, or pleasures.

All this is set against the background of a city and country at a vital moment of its growth, around the end of the 1860s, during Brazil's war with Paraguay, and at the moment when the inevitable end of slavery begins to make itself felt. We watch Rubião, stripped of his money but with his illusions intact, gradually descending into madness and death, believing that the dog, named after its master Quincas Borba, is in fact the philosopher's reincarnation. JG

It was at that time that Rubião astonished all his friends. On the Tuesday following the Sunday of the ride (it was then January, 1870), he asked a barber and hairdresser of Ouvidor Street to send some one to his house to shave him next day at nine o'clock in the morning. A Frenchman, called Lucien, went there, and, according to the orders given to the servant, he was sent to Rubião's study.

'Grr—' growled Quincas Borba, from Rubião's knees.

Lucien bowed to the master of the house; the latter, however, did not see the courtesy, just as he had not heard Quincas Borba's signal. He lay on an elongated couch, quite bereft of his mind, which had broken through the ceiling and had become lost away up in the air. How many leagues had it gone? Neither condor nor eagle could say. On its way to the moon — it only saw the perennial felicity that had showered on it from the cradle, where the fairies had rocked it to sleep, to the shore of Botafogo, where they had taken it, resting on a bed of roses and jasmine. No reverse, no failure, no poverty — a peaceful life, made up of joy, and with more than enough income — it was on its way to the moon!
204–205

# MACHADO DE ASSIS
Joaquim Maria

## The Psychiatrist and Other Stories

This selection of twelve of the best of Machado de Assis's short stories (he wrote altogether almost two hundred), is headed by 'The Psychiatrist'. This is in fact one of his most important works, running to some 50 pages, and less a short story than a comic philosophical tale in the style of Swift or Voltaire. It is set in the last years of Portuguese rule in Brazil, in Itaguaí, a small town not far from Rio de Janeiro. The central character is a doctor, Simão Bacamarte, who decides to carry out a large scale experiment in the town, to define the frontiers of madness: predictably, the results are comic and perverse, ending up with Simão deciding that he himself is the only mad person in the town. On the way, a number of minor charcaters, like Simão's wife, whose exclusive diet of "the wonderful Itaguaí pork" fails in its object of making her pregnant, or the psychiatrist's cowardly side-kick, Crispim Soares, make this a comment on human nature in various of its aspects, including the political.

From the same collection, 'Loose leaves', published in 1882, comes 'The Mirror', another typical mixture of comedy and philosophy: this time it is the essence of human beings, the 'soul' which is the subject. Jacobina is made Second Lieutenant in the (more decorative than useful) National Guard, and, with a handsome uniform. However, in a typical reversal, it turns out that, when he is alone, isolated from others' flattery, it is not his sense of his own identity that saves him, so much as this uniform, without which he would disappear into the mirror. Two other stories, 'Education of a Stuffed Shirt' and 'Final Request', are taken from this, the most comic and fantastic of Machado's collections.

Other stories, in a more realist vein, show Machado's awareness of the brutal side of human nature: 'The Secret Heart' is a study of sadism, climaxing in an unforgettable sense of cruelty wreaked on a mouse. 'The Rod of Justice' and 'Father versus Mother' show this in the context of slavery — they concentrate on figures who are poor, but free, and whose tight, tense situation induces them to vent their frustration on those beneath them, the slaves, with dreadful consequences. His sympathetic and intelligent treatment of women is beautifully displayed in 'A Woman's Arms', 'Admiral's Night', and 'Midnight Mass', the latter a classic of unreliable narration. JG

One day, when preparations were being made for a ball to be held that evening in the town hall, Itaguai was shocked to hear that Simão

Bacamarte had sent his own wife to the asylum. At first everyone though it was a gag of some sort. But it was the absolute truth. Dona Evarista had been committed at two o'clock in the morning.

'I had long suspected that she was a sick woman,' said the psychiatrist in response to a question from Father Lopes... Tonight, however, the full gravity of her illness became manifest. She had selected the entire outfit she would wear to the ball and had it all fixed and ready. All except one thing: she couldn't decide between a garnet necklace and a sapphire necklace. The day before yesterday she asked me which she should wear. I told her it didn't matter, that they were both very becoming. Yesterday at lunch she repeated the question. After dinner she was silent and pensive. I asked her what was the matter. "I want to wear my beautiful garnet necklace, but my sapphire one is so lovely." "Then wear the sapphire necklace." In the middle of the night, about half-past one, I awoke. She was not in bed. I got up and went to the dressing-room. There she sat with the two necklaces, in front of the mirror, trying on first one and then the other. An obvious case of dementia. I had her put away immediately.' 33-34

## MACHADO DE ASSIS
Joaquim Maria

### Yayá Garcia [Yayá Garcia]

A beautiful tribute to the talents, perceptiveness and intelligence of young women who may lack experience but have a precious kind of optimism and energy, Machado slowly builds up a picture of the attractive young Yayá, a charming and affectionate girl, still at school when we meet her.

To begin with we think we're going to read a rather romantic and rose-coloured love story; expecting of course that there might be a few tricks of fate to twist the path of true love — but no reader could ever guess the actual course of events. After his sugary start Machado plunges Yayá and three other contenders in the mating rite into the most extraordinary thwarted situation of mutual dissimulation, manipulation and betrayal.

It is widely agreed that in this early work Machado first demonstrates his genius as a writer and the book's climax in a mad incestual mêlée of jealousy and rivalry is simply very startling. A very deceiving book to begin with that finishes in a narrative whirl. RK

Of the various qualities needed in chess Yayá possessed two of the most essential: quick apprehension and a benedictine patience — qualities equally precious in life, which with its problems and conflicts is itself a game of chess, some games being won, others lost, others drawn. 138

# MELO
Patricia

## The Killer [O Matador]

If you have ever wondered whether a terrible toothache could take you as far as murder than Patricia Melo's novel *The Killer* will confirm your deepest fears. Set in contemporary São Paulo, *The Killer* is Brazil's answer to Tarantino's *Reservoir Dogs* in its depiction of ice cold, detached killers and in its graphic description of random violence. The novel introduces us to Maiquel, a second hand car sales man, who is drawn into a world of spiralling violence after his first visit to the dentist Dr Carvalho. Maiquel initially scoffs at Carvalho' suggestion to kill in return for free dental treatment but gradually finds that killing comes quite easily to him. In fact, it's a hell of a lot easier than selling used cars. His first victim is Suel, a local crook. Much to his surprise Maiquel finds that he is treated like a hero when news of Suel's murder travel around the neighbourhood. And to top it all, Suel's girlfriend, Erica, decides to move in with Maiquel. So, Maiquel decides that all in all murder is not such a bad business. Soon he sets up a contract killer agency together with the bent cop Santana. Things are going very well until Maiquel makes one fatal mistake…

*The Killer* paints a harsh picture of contemporary urban life in Brazil as submerged in corruption, hopelessness and violence. It is the middle classes, as represented by smooth Dr Carvalho, who are the instigators of crime. Poor Maiquel, whose increasing wealth leads him to believe that he is now part of the much aspired to middle-class 'club', doesn't understand that he is merely the readily dispensable instrument of Carvalho's machinations. The latter sees himself as the legislator of local justice by eliminating any possible threat to his comfortable life style. This lynch mob attitude is endorsed by a corrupt police force which applauds the removal of any unwanted criminal element in the neighbourhood. Human lives, as long as they belong to working-class people, are cheap. This is the bitter lesson learned by Maiquel when he kills a young boy who turns out to be the son of a pediatrician. While nobody had previously batted an eyelid, the murder of a middle-class child now provokes a national outcry.

The fact that Patricia Melo works as a screenwriter as well as a novelist comes as no surprise, considering her elliptic sentence structure and her brief, sketchy evocations of location and character. With the detached eye of a camera lens Melo records events without direct commentary, letting the violence speak for itself. AD

I knew that Robinson had died by mistake. Selective killings. Messages, like in Bolivia. Colombia. Venezuela. I was the target. They wanted to kill me because I killed Suel. The wager. My blond hair. Suel turned his back on me and jived off down the street, holding hands with his girl. Go ahead and shoot, he said, kill me from behind. I shot the first round. Suel hit the ground, he must have died instantly. Now they want to kill me. They're going to kill me, I killed Ezequiel. I'm going to tell you something, son. You have lousy teeth. I'm a dentist. I have a problem and you have lousy teeth. We can help one another. You help me, I'll help you. I'll fix your teeth for free and you'll do something for me. Agreed? Ezequiel turned around and saw me. I pulled out the gun, took aim, and bang. I missed with the first shot. Bang. I missed a second time. The third one caught him in the thigh, the fourth one in the chest. He fell, I missed with two more shots, Ezequiel was still alive, I yanked a piece of wood from a fence around a tree and threw myself on him. I hit him in the head, hammered at him, hammered, put out his eyes. I rammed the wooden spike into the rapists' heart, I'd seen this on television, Ezequiel vomited blood and died. I killed Suel. 93

MIRANDA
Ana

## Bay of All Saints and Every Conceivable Sin [Boca do Inferno]

An evocation of the seventeenth-century city of Salvador da Bahia, or 'Bahia', then the capital of Brazil, with its wealth based on sugar cane and the slave trade. Salvador has always been one of Brazil's most important urban centres and the heartland of the African element in her cultural life.

Ana Miranda's book is a colourful historical novel, following the lives of certain leading players in the courtly and ecclesiastical politics of the age, focusing on actual personalities such as the reforming Jesuit Father Antonio Vieira, an important early figure in Brazilian letters and the poet Gregorio de Matos.

Gregorio is a Villonesque character who is as at home in Salvador's brothels as on the heights of Poetic Parnassus. In fact, one of Ana Miranda's themes seems to be that large-scale prostitution, like political corruption, has a long tradition in Brazil, reaching right back into the period of Portuguese rule.

Father Vieira, the foil to the enlightened libertine poet Matos, represents a more sombre social and moral critique of the world around him, including the mistreatment of the American Indian population which at that time was being coerced into forced labour.

Inside this quite extensive book is a wealth of material about life and culture in the Bahia of those days and for the Brazilians, who made it into a bestseller, this is a 'Roots' book, showing the background to much of their history. RK

'Brazil is bring torn apart by the sharp claws of those who govern her,' said Padre Vieira. 'Brazil's problem is that any unjust or arbitrary act carried out here never reaches the right ears in Portugal. Even the thieving doesn't seem to be noticed back in the metropolis. So the people struggle on in the greatest misery. And Brazil is no more than the image and reflection of Portugal, a hotbed of vice and corruption, of infinite extravagance without any financial resources and riddled with all the other contradictions of human nature.' 57

NOLL
João Gilberto

## Hotel Atlantico [Hotel Atlantico and Harmada]

The two novellas that make up this compilation share an identical protagonist and narrative landscape: a nameless, solitary, out-of-work actor endlessly traversing the vast map of Brazil's interior in search of his and his country's true centre, and the warmth and familiarity of human society that everywhere seem lost. In a country of such unwieldy dimensions and cultural diversity, where political chaos and economic turmoil make homelessness the perennial condition for millions, the search for continuity, roots, a sense of place and of identity has been a compulsive obsession. Noll's achievement is to render this powerful, profound allegory of the Brazilian predicament immediately accessible in a cinematic style of rapid but potent images through which familiarity and strangeness, reminiscence and amnesia, meaning and incoherence melt unsettlingly into one another. At the same time his spare, minimalist narrative voice, with its often grotesque self-irony, recalls the tone of the hard-boiled thriller, leading the reader compulsively and relentlessly through his journey into hell and back again.

In the first of the two stories, the protagonist is swept into a doom-laden downward spiral as he is haunted by the imminence of death — from the opening murder at a Rio hotel, through the suicide of a beautiful American fellow-passenger, to his own death on the shores of the Atlantic, following his mysterious amputation and internment in a small-town hospital. The former soap-opera star is reduced to a series of grotesque and disembodied roles that he is obliged to play out with his co-actors — giving the last rites to a dying woman as if he were a messianic seer, or promoting his surgeon's cynical election campaign as the romantic, invalided chaperon to his compassionate daughter.

Only one character — the black nurse whose life's great desire is to see the ocean — offers a redeeming glimpse of genuine companionship and solidarity, helping him escape the nightmare of the hospital to spend his last moments on the seashore, filling his lungs with the Atlantic's air.

*Harmada* finds our anonymous drifter waking up once more, to resume his fitful journey across a dream-like landscape of forests, bars, bus-stations, soup queues and asylums of beggars and orphans. This time, in his painful emergence from the hell of social alienation and anomie, the nameless narrator slowly rediscovers the creative power of language through his vocation as a communicator and artist. Whether as storyteller, preacher, actor or theatre director, it is by voicing, representing and recounting his and other lives that he renders them real, remembered and shared, redeemed from anonymity. At the moving climax of the book his faith in this communicative and redemptive capacity of art is restored to him. The deaf and dumb child shakes him furiously, demanding that he speak. And so, with an unsuspected fluency, he begins to move his hands, inventing, in the silent language of signs, the story of Harmada. DT

As he reaches the centre of the stage the dumb kid stops and utters the same shout that he's uttering now, shaking my arms with a strength you would not have suspected him capable of.

Then I wrench my arms away from his hands.

I light a candle.

The kid stops shouting.

I start making signs with my hands. As if I had always been fluent in the language of the deaf.

I tell a long story which unfolds in Persia, filled with knights, monsters, apparitions at every bend in the road...

A terrible thunderbolt severs in two the child in its mother's arms. The white horse whinnies, in the distance a purplish glow in the sky.

Swashbucklers are hanging by a thread in their duel on the castle walls.

The long lost lady walks into the lake. She drowns. At the bottom of the water she discovers that death is a dream, when beings with no precise anatomy surround her and invite her to take part in a black feast of pebble soft with slime.

The vicissitudes of the hero are so many that the kid sometimes seems to be surrounded by a great selection of treats, not knowing which of them to concentrate on.

Suddenly I feel my hands turning numb with tiredness.

I take my handkerchief out of my pocket.

I wipe the sweat from my hands.

Day is breaking."

# OLINTO
Antonio

## The Water House [A Casa de água]

In *The Water House* and its sequel book *King of Ketu*, Olinto tackles the Afro-Brazilian experience, particularly exploring the connections of Black Brazilians with West Africa, where many originated and from where they were transported to Brazil to be plantation slaves.

*The Water House* is the story of a freed slave making the —journey back to Nigeria to find relatives left behind and their original homeland. It makes it a Brazilian 'Roots' book written years before Alex Hailey's *Roots* which followed the story of a contemporary African-American tracing his family line back to an African ancestor.

Different from *Roots* too is that Olinto tries to stay close to the forms of African speech and oral literature, 'the voices of the people', to tell the story, making it a more poetic, more difficult but also more interesting literary work. RK

I do not know how she spent her last days, I cannot find anything in her memories which sets aside these days from others, each the same as the next, going down to the river, milk and salt corn-cake in the morning, black beans and cabbage at midday, now and then dried salt meat and black beans, conversations about things that hid themselves in the cellar, the *mula-sem-cabeça*, the priest's mistress who, when she was dead, turned into a mule without a head and came out of the cemetery in the middle of the night, dead people who came back to tell you what heaven was like, or hell or purgatory, the little girls playing ring games, here comes Margarida, *Olé Olé Olà*, I am poor, poor, poor, the night fell suddenly and the stars twinkled with happiness, when everything was dark the talking in the kitchen went on until very late, the stove crackling, the lamp lighting the way along the passage full of mystery. But yes, she does remember the last day, or rather not the whole day, but the moment of departure, four horses, her mother, her grandmother, her brother and sister herself and a man who was going to look after them, from early morning... 7

# PIÑON
Nélida

## The Republic of Dreams [A República dos sonhos]

Nélida Piñon's *The Republic of Dreams* is an epic tale of ambition, adventure, desire, and longing. In one sense autobiographical — the author, herself of Galician descent, draws on her own past — this novel traces four generations of a family who leave their native Galicia in Spain in search of a new life in Brazil, the 'Republic of Dreams' of the title. The story opens with the main female protagonist, the elusive matriarch Eulália, preparing for her own death, of which she has had a premonition. Her husband Madruga, the ruthless and ambitious patriarch, is bewildered by his wife's matter-of-fact acceptance of her own impending departure from this life, but finds he is powerless to fight against it. As the family members gather around Eulália's deathbed, the reader is taken back in time to share in four generations of memories, legends and traditions of this family, experiencing, through skillful narrative techniques, both the joys and hardships of life in Brazil, and the promise of greater things to come. As Piñon charts their struggle to reconcile their Spanish past with their Brazilian present, she brings to light burning socio-cultural issues such as the search for identity, social displacement, slavery, political upheaval and the problematics of male-female relationships.

*The Republic of Dreams* is a unique and rich blend of story-telling and actual historical events which is not only enthralling but also provides a very informative introduction to the history of Brazil. Helen Lane's translation of the text is wonderfully readable, and skillfully portrays the emotional and psychological depth of Piñon's characters. This novel is as complex as it is captivating; a challenging and rewarding read for all who embark on this epic adventure. S.Smith

Eulália started to die on Tuesday. Having forgotten the last Sunday dinner, when the family had gathered together around the long table specially made so as to have room enough to receive children and grand-children as guests. At the head, Madruga presided over the festivities and customs that had been a solid tradition in his house ever since his arrival in America. So he listened to those present with a certain boredom, demanding of them their life's blood and appreciation for the platters heaped with fancily garnished dishes.

Eulália allowed her husband to share discrete portions of herself, eager to be off to her room, followed always by Odete, her faithful maidservant. Or to church, still fasting, arriving in time to attend the first Mass, which she never missed, not even for one day.

Near the altar, absorbed in the beads of her rosary and the scent of the lighted candles, she would little by little make the saints and the gold and silver objects part of a reality shaped by her dreams and foreign to ordinary eyes. And when some diffuse and nameless voice was about to suffocate her heart, Eulália hastened to receive, along with the host, memories of Galicia, to which she had not returned for years now. Faint, almost colorless memories, and the words with which to fix them missing. With deep sadness, then, Eulália fortified herself with prayer and her shy smile.

## QUEIROZ
Rachel de

### Dora, Doralina [Dôra, Doralina]

Dora leaves her hostile mother and the family ranch in the wilds of Ceará to follow her heart and find her independence. In the capital Fortaleza she joins a theatre company and journeys with them throughout the North-East, then South through Minas Gerais to Rio de Janeiro, observing the countryside, the audiences and her flamboyant companions along the way, her eventful new life making up for her lonely childhood on the *Fazenda Soledade* ('Loneliness Ranch').

Queiroz portrays both rural and urban Brazil, from desert scrubland to Copacabana beach, her travelling heroine quickly learning to adapt to her new surroundings. No matter where she goes, she never forgets her North-Eastern roots, her accent, local sayings and customs, for they are an important part of her identity. References to the Prestes Column (a legendary "Long March" of leftist rebel soldiers in the mid 1920s), World War Two, and populist President Getúlio Vargas' suicide in 1953, set the scene in historical terms. The period detail of Studebakers, hand-made dresses and soap operas on the radio help bring Dora's world to life for the reader. The novel portrays her search for love, not necessarily to be found in marriage, and the value of friendship. As usual in Rachel de Queiroz's work the female characters are strong and independent (the figure of the independent widow appears frequently) and also lonely.

Dora tells her story in a lively and chatty way, punctuating her observations with exclamations and questions to the reader. Her account jumps backwards and forwards in time as she is reminded of something in the past or gets emotional, mentioning a detail for the first time and whetting the reader's appetite to know more. Highly entertaining throughout, as a good actress should be, she keeps our attention by depicting moments of conflict and tragedy but also lots of comedy, and by describing exciting moments or colourful scenes, such as a rowdy Carnival parade in downtown Rio, a nationalistic show to boost morale during the war, or a packed riverboat navigating the São Francisco river. Dora's eye for touches of beauty, especially in nature, and her sensitivity towards and awareness of the feelings of others are clear from her actions within the text, and from the compelling way she tells her story. CW

Most of what they caught was piranha. I knew piranha very well; in the *sertão* that was what we had mostly. The Sitia stream, a tributary of the Salgado, in turn a tributary of the Jaguaribe, was where all the *sertão* piranhas came from. But ours was a little fish that got no bigger than the palm of one's hand at most; and there were two kinds of them, the white and the black, the black being the more ferocious. When I was a small girl, Senhora sometimes called me a *black piranha* because of what she called my evil nature...

Seu Brandini caught the largest fish of all; the creature writhed on the deck, leaped half a meter in the air and glittered in the sun. Seu Brandini threw himself on top of the fish and held the gills in order not to be bitten (in the *sertão* there is a saying that the piranha bites even after it is dead), and he let out that yell of happiness that was like Tarzan's roar: 'My God, but this is the life!' 155–156

## QUEIROZ
Rachel de

### The Three Marias [As Três Marias]

Rachel de Queiroz was born in 1910 in the interior of the North-Eastern state of Ceará and grew up on her family's ranch in the depths of the *sertão* (the wild backlands), whose landscape and lifestyle are depicted vividly in her work. Her books have a strong sociological content, presenting the trials and tribulations of man's struggle against nature in the unforgiving *sertão*, but from a distinctly female point of view, focusing on the role of women in this very male-oriented and almost feudal environment of powerful landowners, isolated ranches and overworked peasants. She presents the roles that are acceptable to women, and how limited and controlled they are, and she also shows how those who rebel against the norm are punished, ostracized, or regarded as criminal or even insane. She has received critical acclaim and great popularity within her country and in 1977 she was the first woman elected to the Brazilian Academy of Letters.

Queiroz attended a strict convent school in the state capital Fortaleza, undoubtedly the model for the setting of her fourth novel *The Three Marias* (1939). The Marias of the title are Maria Augusta, or 'Guta' (the narrator), Maria José and Maria Glória, three very different characters who were best friends in the convent. The novel tells the story of their school days and then of what happened to each of them when they left, comparing them before and after their emergence into the wider world. Guta has great expectations of life: she wants a career, she hopes to find true love, she longs to travel and have adventures and she is determined to escape from the role of housewife and mother that an unforgiving and moralistic society and a strict Catholic upbringing prescribed for women. She tries constantly to understand the opposite sex and empathises with misfits and rebels who do not conform to society's expectations.

Queiroz's narrator is a close observer of social types and sensitive to body language, with an eye for the beautiful and the ridiculous. Using an uncomplicated style, in the tone of a diary or a conversation between close friends, the narrator confides in the reader, telling of her hopes and dreams, impressions and disappointments and her determination to to strive for independence and fulfillment, despite society's restrictions and reactions. CW

I was eighteen when I started to work, and six months later I had already started to fear getting old without ever knowing what the world was all about.

The world — my thirst for it was great. Not for pleasures, or rather, not solely for pleasures. My soul was like that of the soldier in the folktale of Pedro Malasarte who abandons everything, sets out with his knapsack on his shoulder, experiences hunger and persecutions, walks covered with dust and weariness through strange cities governed by cruel and crafty kings, all plotting his downfall. He, however, a slave to his desire to 'see,' to 'know,' confronts all things, continues eternally in search of the impossible surprise, of things never seen, journeying always ahead, beneath the sun and through peril.

I felt I was like him, that the two of us were brother and sister, the soldier and I, and I was his sister who stayed behind, who could not accompany him, and who held out her arms to him and wept. 69

## RAMOS
Graciliano

### Barren Lives [Vidas secas]

Dating back to 1938 this is one of the all-time great novels of rural existence in Brazil, telling of the life of a small migrant family (and their dog) in the harsh social and ecological conditions of the drought-plagued state of Alagoas. In an elementally sparse ranching landscape of scrubland and marginal pastures Ramos studies his family in separate chapters, one by one, from the leathery, ignorant father down to the most sympathetic member, the family dog and these chapters somehow seem to be exactly the right length. We share the realities of their lives, including a brush with the law, the experience of winter, huddling around the fireplace and then the overwhelming impact of a town on the two little boys visiting one for the first time, kids who have never seen other people before.

Ramos writes with a satisfying simplicity that seems to reflect perfectly the stripped-down lifestyle of his characters, semi-nomadic hired hands who have to live with the bare minimum of things and aspirations. What sets this book apart from other examples of the social realist Regionalist school of writing of the period, though, is his attention to the characters' inner lives, their cultural, linguistic and psychological impoverishment apparently mirroring their material poverty. Through a special technique of indirect reported 'speech-thought', Ramos seems to dramatise the central rhetorical point of the book: can we really communicate with or understand the experience of these people? Their isolation, brutalisation and verbal clumsiness seem to tell us no; but Ramos's novel is, like Fabiano's belief in the power of his wife's words of hope, an act of faith that we, and they, can break the bounds of a familiar but imprisoning existence and reach beyond.

The final fate of this family, poised between the drought that begins the book and the one that ends it is to continue their trek out of the countryside and into the big city, following in the footsteps of so many other poor Brazilians, then and now. *Barren Lives* is a moving and deeply sympathetic but grimly unsentimental short book, with a sweet wry touch; an undoubted and enjoyable classic that produced an equally classic screen version by *Cinema Novo* pioneer Nelson Pereira dos Santos. RK and DT

Indignant at the injustice, the boy left the house, crossed the yard and took refuge under the dry catingueira trees beside the empty pond.

The dog was his companion in that hour of trial. She had been stretched out beside the stones on which Vitória did the cooking, drowsing in the heat, waiting for a bone. In all probability she wouldn't get one, but she believed in bones and she found the state of torpor enjoyable. She stirred a bit from time to time, raising to her mistress black eyes shining with confidence. Having accepted the idea that there might be a bone in the kettle, she was not going to let anybody or anything disturb her modest hopes. She got an occasional kick for no reason at all. The kicks were to be expected and did nothing to dispel the vision of the bone. 56

# RAMOS
Graciliano

## Childhood [Infância]

Halfway between memoirs and a novel, *Childhood* (1945) recounts the author's formative years in the interior of the north-eastern state of Alagoas between 1892 and 1904. Although Ramos provides a colourful portrait of small town life and characters in the *sertão*, we are repeatedly reminded that this was a harsh and often brutal world, overshadowed by the perennial fear of drought and characterised by violence, illness, poverty and migration.

Consisting of thirty-nine short chapters, *Childhood* charts the progress of young Graciliano as he gradually and painfully comes to realise that he has a vocation as a writer. His struggle, as he grapples with the difficulty of achieving literacy in a repressive elementary school, forms the centrepiece of the book. It is Ramos' austere and forbidding father who rather surprisingly provides the impetus for his son's literary breakthrough by encouraging him to read aloud, thereby fuelling his growing thirst for knowledge. *Childhood* alternates between scenes of claustrophobic rural life and poetic and dream-like interludes. Its fragmentary, episodic nature and rather jolting, detached, narrative is lightened by occasional bursts of wry humour. As in several of his other works, Ramos' chief concern revolves around the linguistic and emotional barriers that prevent meaningful communication between us all. SS

I remember my first bath. In the heat, the cold jet would caress us. Sr. Filipe Benício scrubbed himself with soap and became the colour of a sugar- plum. He would shake part of his body as though he wished to untie it. Diving in the shallow tank, he panted like an animal. He would get up, rid of the suds, fresh and clean. His long moustaches spread out, white; the tangled hair on his belly, also white, surprised me. I didn't think that such hairy people existed.

From the trough the water overflowed and ran freely over the cultivated land, moistening the field of enormous sugar-cane, the only one on these farms. Once the humidity ended, the backlands emerged, to start with uncertain and monotonous, filled with insignificant palm and cashew trees, then dry and yellow, covered with cactus, bones and pebbles. There crept the famished and dirty creatures who sold baskets of wild plums and small game at the fair. In times of scarcity they lived off this, and since scarcity was frequent, they migrated and ended in misery. 111

# RAMOS
Graciliano

## São Bernardo [São Bernardo]

Graciliano Ramos was one of a number of North-eastern novelists whose writings in the 1930s and 40s were instrumental in drawing attention to their native region. Paulo Honório, the narrator of *São Bernardo* (1934), is a ruthless, self-made man who rises from humble origins to achieve his dream of owning a large *fazenda* (estate) in the North-eastern state of Alagoas. His triumph is characterised by the murder of a rival, a neighbouring landowner named Mendonça, and yet Ramos portrays Paulo Honório as the product of his environment, a society pervaded by endemic corruption, where only the strong survive. Despite his tyrannical behaviour, Ramos makes it clear that Paulo Honório is a man whose power and influence is ultimately based on weak foundations, for his total distrust of all around him leads directly to his eventual downfall.

His marriage to Madalena, a poor schoolteacher with a social conscience and an independent spirit, proves to be the prelude to his descent into a fury of self-destructive jealousy, which eventually leads to his wife's suicide. Paulo Honório's recognition of his failure to communicate with Madalena, and its contribution to her death, leaves him at the novel's conclusion largely abandoned by friends and family, consumed by self-loathing and regret as he contemplates a lonely end to his embittered life.

Ramos' unsentimental, powerful novel is driven along by a compressed, urgent style that mirrors the terse, impatient nature of its narrator. With references to the political turbulence which accompanied the rise to power of dictator Getúlio Vargas in 1930, Ramos draws a vivid picture of a conservative, rural Northeast, symbolised by the character of Paulo Honório, who is unwilling or unable to come to terms with changing times. SS

Next day, Saturday, I killed the sheep for the voters. Sunday evening, as he was returning from the election, Mendonça was shot in the chest and bit the dust there and then, on the road close to Bom-Sucesso. Today the spot is marked by a cross with one of its arms missing. At the time of the murder I was in town talking to the parish priest about the church I intended to build in S. Bernardo. In the future, that is, provided business progressed satisfactorily.

'How terrible!' said Father Silvestre when they brought the news. 'Did he have any enemies?'

'Enemies! Did he have any enemies! As thick as lice. Well, what about it, Father Silvestre? How much did you say a bell costs?' 30–31

# RIBEIRO
Darcy

## Maíra [Maíra]

Published in 1976, *Maíra* dramatises one of the most urgent social issues of the late twentieth century: the survival of traditional peoples and cultures, especially the tribal Amerindians, in the face of globalisation and industrial development. Ribeiro was well qualified to write about the Brazilian Indians; during fifty odd years of a distinguished career as an anthropologist (as well as educator and politician), he researched among and wrote on numerous tribal groups in Brazil. In 1970 he published *The Indians and Civilization*, a masterfully comprehensive work originally commissioned by UNESCO to assess, in the words of the book's subtitle 'the integration of the indigenous populations into modern Brazil'. What in fact emerged was a depressing account of the failure of any such assimilation, and it is that failure which lies at the heart of *Maira*.

The story of the central character Isaías Avá is based on the real case of a Bororo Indian from Matto Grosso who, in 1910, at the age of twelve, was removed from his community by Salesian missionaries and eventually sent to Rome and Paris to become a priest. On attempting to resume his tribal role as hunter and farmer by marrying a Bororo woman, he discovered that he had become alienated from the society of his birth. For the rest of his life he occupied a cultural and psychological limbo between two worlds.

The real achievement of *Maira*, though, is its location of this individual struggle for personal self-integration within a complex yet skilfully constructed picture of Amazonian society and of the political, economic and cultural forces trying to transform it. The voices of the principal characters in the drama each contribute their own perspective: the voice of tribal tradition, recounting the story of the creation of the world, and the beautiful funeral ritual of the Mairun chief; the voice of the river trader Juca, himself a detribalised Indian determined to seduce the remainder of his people into the economic slavery to which the local non-Indian population is condemned; the voice of the police inspector sent to investigate the mysterious death of a white woman, and who in the process reveals the negligent role played by FUNAI (the Brazilian government organization that deals with Amerindians) as intermediary between the Indians and white society; and the voice of Isaías himself, resigned to the eventual disappearance of the Mairuns as the conclusion of an inexorable process of acculturation.

The chapters devoted to the Mairun culture and mythology are the most memorable, not least because of the painful irony they bring to the whole question of the survival of the tribal communities. For the strength of the Indians' highly sophisticated systems of kinship, social organisation and cosmology, their self-containment and self-sufficiency, also contain the seeds of their vulnerability. The duality that divides the Mairuns into two clans, and thereafter penetrates every aspect of tribal life, must necessarily include the duality of within/

without, here/there, Indian/white. Most significantly, it extends to the book's title, whose several related meanings — Maira the universal creator hero of Tupi mythology; Maira the 'transformer'; Maira the bringer of civilization; Maira the foreigner; Maira the white man — attest to the Indians' high expectations of a society that has not proved itself worthy of them. DT

But soon the heavier rains fall, raining for many days, weeks, and months. The world then seemed to dissolve under the mantle of widespread water. Black clouds darken the horizons; as they break, rain pours in white curtains on to the thatch of roofs, mud unto the dancing ground. The people, consumed by sadness, huddling around little fires, now are eating dry cassava bread or roast or boiled potatoes, almost always without meat or fish, and are drinking nothing but plain cassava beer. Mosquitoes come out and multiply. Fierce midges, gnats, and punkies sting, annoy. They are the lords of the world. The beaches disappear, inundated by the cold and turbid water of the *paraná*. With them fish, birds, and large and small game also disappear.

So it was for months until little by little the joyfulness of summer began to return. This year the first to arrive were the spotless white ibis and the dusky herons, serene in flight, perching on the crowns of trees, afraid of dirtying their feet. Then came the toucans and their cousins, the toucanets and, finally, flocks of macaws and parrots. All life renews itself.

# RIBEIRO
João Ubaldo

## An Invincible Memory [Viva o povo brasileiro]

João Ubaldo Ribeiro's *An Invincible Memory* promises us something that contemporary Brazilian fiction has tended to shy away from, but which is nevertheless an endeavour worth defending: a coherent and meaningful vision of his country's historical experience 'from below', challenging the 'Great Men' theory of Brazilian history 'as it was taught to me in school' (to quote the dust jacket). Indeed, the novel's moral weight undoubtedly derives from its identification with the oppressed of Brazil and its insistent call for their liberation.

But *An Invincible Memory* doesn't so much offer the Brazilian people a way out of their oppression, as condemn them to an eternal search for a mysterious national consciousness whose discovery is forever postponed. As one of the book's heroes, General Patrício, reveals in the closing pages: 'You'll only be able to be anything after you are you!'. Maybe we shouldn't be surprised that Ribeiro's characters make little progress in their striving for a sense of identity, given the contradictory, ambiguous and ultimately indeterminate nature of this idea on which the entire novel rests. 'Long live the Brazilian People!' is the ubiquitous slogan which the plot's two entangled dynasties of masters and slaves struggle to interpret for themselves. But who is the Brazilian People if, as Ribeiro rightly suggests, the ruling, Europhile elite of sugar-planters and slave-owners has no legitimate claim to the title? For the visionary militia commander, Maria da Fé, the descendent of an Indian *mestiça* ('mixed race' individual*)*, a Dutch soldier, an emancipated slave and a tyrannical baron, the Brazilian People is 'the dispossessed, the oppressed and the wronged' or, in a rare moment of precision, all the 'workers' of nineteenth century society: the artisans, tradesmen, farmers, millers, innkeepers and musicians.

However, as the blood of one dynasty contaminates that of the other, and individuals even renounce family loyalties to fight alongside the rebels, it becomes clear that Ribeiro cannot and does not want to make up his mind: blurring the boundaries between class and nation, his notion of the spirit of the people is less a matter of social identity and more an attitude of mind, a belief in freedom. Thus the members of the mysterious Brotherhood are only recognisable by an intuitive sixth sense: 'There was something in certain people, the way they walked, the way they talked, their type of voice'.

Meanwhile, by reducing a complex history of class, ideological and ethnic antagonisms to a single idealistic struggle for national identity, Ribeiro has effectively exchanged one set of myths, those of racial degeneracy and pathological underdevelopment, for another — Gilberto Freyre's myth of *mestiçagem*. The *mestiça* heroine, Maria da Fé, embodies the spirit of a permanent struggle for social and racial democracy, in which contradiction, plurality and difference are the vitalising ingredients of a dynamic, but essentially integrated, harmonious society. Outright elitism is exchanged for a more subtle, and sinister, populism, whose exhortation to freedom becomes an end in itself, because there is no real end.

This is the central message of a novel that, for all its wealth of material, carefully dated chapter titles and panoramic sweep of Brazilian history, is in essence profoundly anti-historical. It is not by chance that seventeen of the book's twenty chapters are concerned solely with events from the nineteenth century. Besides marking the independence and consolidation of the Brazilian nation-state, this is the period in which the notion of a Brazilian 'people', let alone a working class, with distinct common interests, is most problematic, given the centrality of slavery to the country's economy and society. Da Fé's list of 'workers' corresponds much more closely to a pre-industrial petite bourgeoisie, straddling an uncertain, ambiguous terrain between the slaves, whose material oppression they often shared, and the masters, on whose patronage they were socially dependent.

Ribeiro's version of the 'people's' democratic struggle therefore remains, for the most part, rather distant from the new and complex social reality of twentieth century industrial Brazil, which merits only two chapters. Stopping short of the exciting new popular and working class movements that have remerged since the 1970s, the book instead retreats to the safety of a mythical Golden age and place, the nineteenth century North-east, which stands for a timeless national-popular consciousness. A succession of slave rebellions, Liberal revolts, regional uprisings and messianic movements is subsumed, often by means of contrived circumstantial connections, into the history of the (Bahian) Brazilian people's search for its identity, losing in the process their specific social and political character. Most important of all, in Ribeiro's essentially Hegelian view of the struggle between oppressor and oppressed, it is only the people's consciousness which is ever transformed. Moments before his death, General Patrício speaks of the Spirit of Man, which 'yearns for perfection, that is to say, Good'.

'Souls do not learn anything, but they dream uncontrollably', we read in the first chapter of *An Invincible Memory*, as the spirit of the Brazilian people resumes its journey of self-realisation, a journey that, if Ribeiro is to be believed, is likely to remain unfinished for a long time to come. DT

Lord in heaven, who was that statue of glory, beautiful in countenance and speech, if not the warrior Maria da Fé, bursting forth through incomprehensible arts, emerging from the clothes of a mean looking captain like an obscure worm turning into a triumphant butterfly, shining like a sun amid all the rain, coming to unleash the pride that had been rotting away in their fearful hearts? Here she is in flesh and bone, not a legend but a truth you could touch, not distant but near, leading not soldiers but a squad of militiamen — the Militia of the People, whom so many had heard of and so few had seen. 288

# RIBEIRO
João Ubaldo

## The Lizard's Smile [O Sorriso do lagarto]

João Ubaldo Ribeiro's playfully imaginative novel is set in his native Bahia and incorporates a heady mix of philosophical ideas revolving around the classic literary device of a love triangle. The reader is swiftly introduced to the central characters — a trio of angst-ridden middle-class individuals, none of whose private lives matches their public personae. Ângelo Marcos, a prominent politician and ostensibly a pillar of the community, is revealed to be a duplicitous, adulterous tyrant. Ângelo's wife, Ana Clara, bored and trapped in her stultifying marriage, is encouraged by her flirtatious friend Bebel to seek a liberating love affair, and in the process discovers a hidden talent for writing trashy novels. Completing the triangle is João Pedroso, an alcoholic biologist turned fishmonger whose chance meeting and subsequent relationship with Ana Clara sets in motion a chain of events that have profound implications for all involved. All three characters are reluctant to confront their respective inner demons and Ribeiro unravels their complexities utilising a skilful combination of mordant humour and genuine pathos.

Interwoven within the novel's dramatic fabric are a series of philosophical musings on topics such as contemporary sexual and political morality, evolution, race, and religion. Ribeiro deftly mixes all these diverse ingredients into a hugely entertaining book brimming with unexpected twists and turns and large doses of eroticism, which is only slightly weakened by a rather unconvincing subplot concerning genetic engineering. SS

Even so, perhaps he could still pray. Wasn't there such a thing as the infinite mercy of God? Infinite, infinite; one must focus on that word. Infinite. Didn't such mercy exist? It did, it really did. It was true that he had prayed so much, before the result of the biopsy had arrived, had prayed so much that once he'd felt himself almost levitate after spending ten minutes kneeling in fervent prayer in his office at the Ministry, and then got to his feet convinced that the report would be negative. For some hours he reflected confidently about how it had all been nothing but a scare, a way of shaking him and forcing him to take a new tack in his life, to observe certain things, take a fresh look at certain habits and practices. After all, there was truly great wisdom in the saying that God writes straight with crooked lines; life really is the only great school, and God is good. For that very reason he almost cursed God and all the saints when he saw, in a book whose cover was embossed with a horrible crab transfixed by a dagger, the macabre words that continued to pursue him like some funereal verse, written by a computer printer: EPIDERMOID CARCINOMA OF THE ANAL CANAL. 39

# RIBEIRO
João Ubaldo

## Sergeant Getulio [Sargento Getúlio]

Sergeant Getulio is a man with a mission — to escort a left-wing political prisoner across the wild, hostile backlands of Brazil's North-East and deliver him, alive, to the coastal town of Aracaju, where he awaits his trial and probable execution. Whether or not Getulio completes this mission becomes a dramatic test of his *own* survival, as the personification of an entire culture of brutally *machista* individualism and uncompromising order. For he is beset by pressures that seem intent on undermining his purpose and raison d'être — the vacillations of the government, which announces half-way through the journey that the prisoner must be released, pursuing Getulio as a criminal deserter when he refuses to comply; the urge to anticipate the court's judgement and execute his own sentence of justice on the man who comes to symbolise all his loathing and contempt for the values of the wider world; and the power of the desert itself, inspiring both love and hatred in Getulio, reminding him of his encroaching old age and mortality, with its twin options: voluntary retirement with a wife and family, or a sudden, violent death at the head of some apocalyptic army of latter-day bandits.

*Sergeant Getulio* stands in the best tradition of North-Eastern fiction — punctuated by Graciliano Ramos's *Barren Lives* and Guimarães Rosa's *The Devil to Pay in the Backlands* — in its exploration of the culture and mentality of the rural interior through the medium of its own oral language, at once primitive and severe, rich and lyrical. The only voice is that of Getulio's rambling monologue, heard by his literally captive audience and by the few companions on his mission, living and dead. In this near seamless monologue he reveals the social, psychological and emotional anatomy of a people struggling to assert its identity as its traditional world is eroded and collapses about it. Like the excellent film based on it, this book poses an unforgettable challenge — to recognise a humanity in Getulio's cruel rage, in his violent refusal to surrender to anonymity and oblivion. DT

All houses look like platefuls of food even if it is manioc flour mush. This Hudson, when it broke down for lack of gasoline, I gave it a good look and thought it was quite a monarch of a thing , because it necessitated the putting of gasoline in it by us and we used up all the cans and I wonder where the hell we are in this world. To tell the truth, I do know, but I see that walking is the thing that must be done and the junk opens his mouth and says that he cannot walk. And I say, yes, you can walk. Otherwise I will do the worst things to you, don't get fresh. But I really wouldn't do anything, with all this tiredness and even my jacket I took off because it weighed on me, I can barely carry my weapon and Amaro his, he actually likes it very much, he does everything short of kissing it, in fact I think he does, at night when no one is watching he gives it a few kisses. I know he polishes it with the cloth he got from the car. I stood looking at this car, which is new but has long become old, and I remained looking at it, all cold. It stood there, dead. Amaro still lifted the hood and looked inside, a heap of parts it had inside, all still; even Hudsons die. Then what is left for Amaro is the little two-barrelled thing, which he strokes and polishes and sniffs and when he leans it against something he pulls back and makes it stand on its butt and takes to gazing at it like a father gazes at a daughter. 93–94

# SCLIAR
Moacyr

## Ballad of the False Messiah [Balada do falso Messias]

In *Ballad of the False Messiah* we get eleven of Moacyr Scliar's best stories, mostly on Jewish or Jewish-Brazilian themes. The title piece is a bittersweet, brief re-telling of the Shabbatai Zevi story 'transferred to a Jewish agricultural colony in Southern Brazil. Shabbatai Zevi was one of the 'False Messiahs' who appeared during a desperate period of Ashkenazi Jewish history in the sixteenth and seventeenth centuries, promising to lead his compatriots out of *tzuresdike golus* (painful exile) to dwell with the Lord in *Eretz Yisroel* (the land of Israel). Needless to say it didn't quite turn out as prophesised, and nor did the high hopes of the Jewish colonies in Brazil.

'Don't Release the Cataracts' is a snippet of black humour, mild and Thurberesque like many of Scliar's pieces. 'New Year, New Life' is more of the same, and satirizes the Yiddish saying *'nayes yor, nayes lebn'* (New year, new life) with the story of a 'bum', a madcap 'hippie' who scrapes along in idleness and cupidity. 'The Scalp' is a very strange little story, very short but rich in its exploration of resentments based on social class, gender and even looks... While in 'The Spider' we catch another whiff of ingrained resentment, surely a very common emotion, here between a woman and her porky lover who bribes her affections with snacks from his grocery store. Moving away from the theme of 'love', in 'Eating Paper' Scliar manages to be funny, ironic and noirish on the subject of Life Insurance.

'The Evidence' is a thoughtful tale of cruelty and avidity, where 'invisible currents of hatred, of repressed hostility... flow in the moments of silence' while 'The Offerings of the Dalial Store' is a surprising story of everyday perversion but also somehow magical, while the final longer piece here, 'The Short-Story writers' is a writer's self-parodic investigation on every possible type of short story writer including Helena, a manicurist short story writer; 'The characters created by Helena, a manicurist, were fingernails: "I write about what I know", she would say... RK

I caught sight of short-story writer Volmir. Whenever short-story writer Volmir wanted to write, he would closet himself in his study for two or more days. When he reappeared, he was changed but happy. He would invite his wife and daughters into his study, where they would stand around the desk upon which lay the typed pages held together with a brand-new paper clip. Full of jubilant respect, they would stare at the short story for several minutes.

'What's the title?' they would ask, and when the short-story writer disclosed it, they would hug one another, overcome by joy. Short-story writer Murtinho organized the production of his short stories in accordance with the assembly-line principle: outlines in the top drawer, half-finished short stories in the second drawer, finished short stories in the third drawer. Short-story writer Manduca, quite soused, hugs me whimpering:

'1 can only write under the influence of bennies and lately they haven't had any effect... I've been taking the weirdest things, I've even tried deodorant...' 'The Short-story Writers' 47

## SCLIAR
Moacyr

### The Centaur in the Garden [O Centauro no jardim]

Moacyr Scliar is a Brazilian Jew, and says that the spirit of his writing lies in his early background: he went to a Yiddish High School in Porto Alegre. 'As much as possible I live in peace with my Jewishness', he says. 'I have extracted from it what it has of the best: fantasy, ethical substance, and above all, humour... melancholy, bittersweet, the humour of the persecuted fighting against desperation'. All this is much in evidence in *Centaur in the Garden* which contains perhaps Scliar's most adventurous metaphor for the difficulty or complexity of being Jewish in Brazil, a country that has not found much cultural space for its minorities.

A centaur is a mythological creature, it appears no where else but in Greek mythology, but the centaur in *this* book is Jewish, and lives in

Brazil. This is upsetting for the poor centaur, Guedali, who is indisputably real, so shockingly real, that when he came into the world his mother entered a catatonic state... He is of course a mixture of things, with several natures dictating his behaviour. Desperate for answers, he can never find them in any one camp alone: reality, fantasy; being a man, a horse; an intellectual, instinctive; Brazilian, Jewish....

Guedali's parents are Jewish immigrants from Russia, who have come to Brazil to escape the pogroms; 'A pogrom: drunken Cossacks would invade the village, charging on their crazed horses against children and old citizenry, loot and burn the village, and then disappear, leaving the echoes of screams and neighing behind them in the tormented night.' However, Guedali himself is born in Brazil, but raised in the Jewish tradition. This does not make things easier for his parents, who, respecting the faith, have to convince the *mohel* to come and circumcise the half-boy half-horse.

Luckily his parents are farmers, living isolated from any neighbours so Guedali can run free in the woods. He is able to gallop about satisfactorily, but he is never able to shake off his anxiety about being different despite the love and acceptance of his family. And what's more, he is forced to follow his animal impulses, which at times are at variance with his human reasoning: very alienating for him, as he cannot *explain* to his family his irrational horse's instincts. Add to this the complication that he is an intellectual beast, encouraged by his Jewish parents to read, cultivate his mind: 'Read, my son, read,' my mother would say. 'The things you learn no one can take away from you. It doesn't matter that you have a handicap, the important thing is to educate yourself.' He reads voraciously, looking for signs everywhere that he is somehow to be explained. He reads everything, from the history of his people, to Marx and Freud. But he finds nothing. No text comes anywhere near to solving the riddle for him; nor can they attempt to satisfy him with their questions so far from his own.

Finally, he decides to leave the comfort of being loved and accepted and search for answers. He meets a centauress, Tita, surprisingly, but this still brings no answers. Now they are two to struggle for the answer to the riddle of their existence. Together — in denial of their equine nature — they successfully undergo an operation by a Moroccan doctor who normally performs sex-change operations. Eventually they become fully human and live the normal life they had always yearned for.

They slowly come to the realisation that 'normal' life can be quite boring, lacking in the fantasy it once had when they were different, when they were beings belonging to mythology. Being fully human only leaves them thirsting for the freedom associated with being an animal. The book, written in the 1980s, presents them and their friends as dull young yuppies, with unadventurous tastes. But Guedali describes himself at this point as 'a crippled centaur, deprived of its equine body', 'a human being trying to liberate himself from his fantasies'.

Scliar combines the problematic of Jewish identity in Brazil with a vivid exploration of society's sexual mores and contradictions through the cipher of Guedali's animality and animal lack of inhibition. A book full of humour and surprising beauty as in Guedali's encounter with another legendary and sexually potent creature, the Sphinx named 'Lolah', half-woman, half-lioness… AC

Once more I hesitated. But I couldn't see her body: it was an amorphous mass hidden in shadow. Besides, I was already here. Why not? I asked myself. Why not?

I went closer. She seemed unaware of my presence; she was lying down, and remained very still. With trembling fingers I opened the door of the cage and went in. I lay down beside her, stroked her face, her breasts. And her body. Her lioness's body. My God, my God, my God!

I had already seen great felines at close quarters when I was in the circus. I had of course held cats on my lap. But I had never touched a lioness…. what voluptuous opulence, the soft fur stood up at my touch, powerful masses of muscle rippled beneath the skin like startled little rabbits under a rug. Her tail rolled up, tense and vibrating.

She turned to face me. The desire that rose from that powerful body engulfed her, one could see; she could barely tolerate it. There was anguish in her eyes, passion of course, but anguish too, in her dilated nostrils and glistening teeth.

'Come,' she whispered.

I was trembling so hard I could barely get my clothes off. There was a terrible moment of hesitation. She was still lying down: how should I go about it? But I knew, something inside me knew. I mounted her from behind, stroking her breasts, kissing her neck hungrily, and penetrating her as a lion would have. She bit my arms as lionesses do lions. And moaned, and cried out so much that I had to put my hand over her mouth for fear of the doctor hearing us.

The copulation was short, the orgasm, colossal. Mountains of Tunisia! What an orgasm that was! You know nothing, oh mountains, if you have never known an orgasm like that!

When it was over we lay on the floor of the cage, gasping.

Little by little I got myself together, began to emerge from the depths of that dark and turbulent sea. Only then did I realize that something was pinning me down by the neck.

It was her left paw. Cautiously, I lifted it off me with a disagreeable thought: if Lolah were to have one of her temper tantrums just now...

'Guedali', she murmured. 'Guedali, my love. Thank you, Guedali.'

I kissed her, went out of the cage, dressed and sneaked back to my room as stealthily as I had come. 173–174

## SCLIAR
Moacyr

### The Enigmatic Eye [O Olho enigmatico]

*Enigmatic Eye* is a short story collection, in fact a collection of very short stories. The best pieces here, the title story for example, are startling and suggestive; time-delayed depth charges to go off in a readers consciousness years later.... 'Inside my dirty head — the Holocaust' is a story on five or six things we know about the Holocaust and some that even now we'd rather not know... On the other hand you could read 'Among the Wise Men' and discover the meaning of fish, read 'The Conspiracy' and discover the inner formula of all political systems. 'The Prodigal Uncle' tests the saying 'blood is thicker than water' while 'Root Canal Treatment' explores existential anxiety rather than dentistry.

'A Brief History of Capitalism' involves a Communist car mechanic, he's no good at his job but does it to because he wants to get his hands dirty and be a proletarian. It's a wonderfully unpredictable piece with an ending that flies like an arrow for the mind to follow. 'A Public Act' is a succinct comment on war and violence while 'Burning Angels' is a little sick-tinted spin on religion and morality. 'Free Topics' is an acid fragment of 'reality programming' while 'The Candidate' is a knowing little satire on the cynicism of political life in Brazil (and elsewhere). 'General Delivery' is a beautiful story about ugliness while 'In the Submarine Restaurant' is all 'noises off' an '*exercice de style*' à la Raymond Queneau. 'Peace and War' is an ironic ambush of our sense of everyday reality as is, in a more sinister way 'The Blank' about a murderer who excises the uncomfortable memory of his murdering; does that make him typically human? The auto-censure of memory must be a one of our survival mechanisms. 'Many Many Meters above good and evil' defies our expectations at every turn. Excellent.

A fascinating series of flashes from an inquiring, agile mind. RK

My father was a Communist and a car mechanic. A good Communist, according to his comrades, but a lousy mechanic according to consensus. As a matter of fact, so great was his inability to handle cars that people wondered why he had chosen such an occupation. He used to say it had been a conscious choice on his part; he believed in manual work as a form of personal development, and he had confidence in machines and in their capability to liberate man and launch him into the future, in the direction of a freer, more desirable life. Roughly, that's what he meant. 45

## SCLIAR
Moacyr

### The Gods of Raquel [Os deuses de Raquel]

Scliar seems to have found a wonderfully eccentric and essential way of talking about 'being Jewish in Brazil'. As a society that is both Catholic, (mildly) nationalist and mostly focused on its Western-European and African roots it is perhaps a rather complex place for a clear and self-confident Jewish sense of self to exist. Such is Scliar's argument, at least. All the book's protagonists and especially the Raquel of the title, a stubborn and funny girl and later young woman, struggle to live as Jews in the provincial Brazil of the 1950s, specifically the Southern city of Porto Alegre.

The origins of Raquel's problems might lie as well with the point of view of her father, a snobbish intellectual Hungarian Jew who draws a very sharp line between himself — assimilated (his intellectual obsession is that not particularly Jewish subject, Latin), from a wealthy background — and what he calls 'ghetto Jews', who, in his view, tend to poverty, speak Yiddish and come from Poland. The result of this attitude is to send Raquel to a convent school where she experiences an intense adolescent religious confusion interpretable as a individualistic form of rebellion against being Jewish in a Catholic environment.

After the convent she falls into an insensate, very physical love-affair with a motor-mechanic, which seems like another confused and passionate attempt to negotiate a coherent world for herself between the various prohibitions of Catholicism, her father's arid snobbery and her mother's more traditional Jewish position.

One has a powerful and haunting sense of Raquel's loneliness, her combined sentimental and spiritual homelessness, the solitude of the detached Jew in a Christian world with its own foibles about difference, but also the loneliness of a person who is different, highly interior and not understood or recognised by others.

Apart from Raquel's crisis-ridden existence and its rehearsal of Jewish identity issues in Latin America *The Gods of Raquel* contains splendid glancing portraits of Brazilian city neighbourhoods and middle-class seaside resorts; Scliar is economical and telling in his writing and he brings this particular book to a quite indescribable and very beautiful close with a passage of old-fashioned spiritual redemption. RK

Sleep wasn't always good. It wasn't good because the sea, roiled by the teeming billions of tiny creatures in its cold, dark water, would not remain quiet. The seasoned vacationers at the resort barely paid any attention to the sea at all, it was only to reassure themselves — if they woke up wondering, Where are we? Who are we? — that they were in Tramandaí, that it was three o'clock in the morning, and that everything was all right. 96

## SCLIAR
Moacyr

### Max and the Cats [Max e os felinos]

*Max and the Cats* is perhaps Scliar's most genial book, written with charm and simplicity, that takes a serious enough subject (forced emigration and making a life in a new continent) but treats it in a surprising, sometimes fantastical way. Max's cats are all 'big cats' and make up quite a strange zoo of creatures; a stuffed tiger that lurks in the store room of his fathers furrier's shop in 1930s Berlin, a hungry Jaguar he has to share a lifeboat with after a shipwreck when he flees Germany for Porto Alegre, and a wild *Onça* — a kind of Brazilian panther — who is entirely imaginary but still germane to the story.

Each big cat symbolizes a stage of his life, each stage as threatening and dangerous in its way as a wild cat but which Max nevertheless manages to escape from. *Max and the Cats* is a real adventure story, as befits a tale of tigers, jaguars and panthers, even though its protagonist is definitely a wimp; when he's shipwrecked his first reaction is to have a good cry. Perhaps though it is this wimpiness that makes the episode of being adrift on the high seas with the jaguar all the more dramatic and surprising. Surprising too is Max's subsequent incarnation as a ferocious Nazi-baiter when he takes on a complacent German war criminal who, like many of his compatriots, has found it 'more convenient' to live in South America after 1945.

*Max and the Cats* is in fact a beautiful, often funny, fable about Nazism (!), Jewish redemption, revenge and, finally, peace. RK

But it was impossible for Max to forget that afternoon in the stockroom. He was always daydreaming about the young woman and would write her passionate letters-which he would promptly destroy — until finally, unable to bear it any longer, he went to see her at her house. Frida, all smiles, received him without rancor, as if nothing had happened. She asked after his father, the store, even the tiger. Then, on an impulse they embraced; they made love on the sofa in the living room, oblivious to the presence of her aunt, a deaf and blind old woman who was sitting in a rocking chair, intoning old Tyrolean songs. 11

## SCLIAR
Moacyr

### The One-Man Army [O Exército de um homem só]

*One-Man Army* starts with a brief run-down of the origins of the Jewish population in Scliar's hometown Porto Alegre; they were escapees from Baron Rothchild's agricultural colonies, designed to re-settle the 'surplus Jews' of the violently anti-Semitic Tsarist Empire.

Mayer Guinzburg is one these ex-colonists, and typical of Scliar's over-the-top but sympathetic heroes; is ultimately defeated by the conundrum of integrating his Jewish identity and 'backstory' with life in Brazil.

His particular gate out of the everyday is his dream of creating 'New Birobidjian' in Brazil. 'Old' Birobidjian was a Jewish settlement created under the auspices of the Communists in the Soviet Far East, near the Amur river. Supposedly a national home for Russia's Jews its actual history was a sad mixture of frustrated idealism and political cynicism. Mayer's New Birobidjian though is a subtle means of talking about the Messianic and Utopian impulse in twentieth Century Jewish history.

The book is very much a gentle satire on the dream of Communism in young Jewish hearts in the 1930s. It's also a gentle satire on Jewish obsessions in general, as in the very funny episode where Scliar puts two Jewish manias back to back; the taboo on pork and the transcendent force of motherlove...

Meyer's favourite phrase is 'At this moment we begin the building of a new society...' and we get to witness the 'creation; of various separate attempts at New Birobidjian with echoes of Orwell's *Animal Farm* (whose comic qualities were often lost when read in a harsh cold war context) when the only other denizens of are 'Comrade Pig', 'Comrade Hen' and 'Comrade Goat'. Meyer is by nature an autocrat which of course has its effect on the egalitarian society he is supposed to be creating in miniature.

On the other hand Scliar is also presenting us with a man of hope in the sense that Meyer rejects a life based on only the concerns of today, daring to look into the future and trying to be a pioneer and a prophet. He turns us to a remark of another Russian-born visionary, cinéaste Andrei Tarkovsky; 'It's far harder to maintain a high moral state than to vegetate in insignificance.' RK

Mayer Guinzburg discourses on New Birobidjian; the crops, the factories, the Palace of Culture. he ends his speech in a firm, calm voice: 'At this moment we begin the building of a new society.'

They shove a tall bamboo pole into the ground to be used as a flagpole, and on it they raise Lydia's colorful kerchief, seeing .that New Birobidjian doesn't have a flag of its own yet. Marc Friedmann opens the door with difficulty. The house is empty except for an old brown leather couch. The floorboards are strewn with dead insects. Mayer Guinzburg immediately divides the group into several committees: the Cleaning-up Committee; the Food Committee; and the Political Studies Committee, of which he is the chairman. How will they spend the rest of the day? 'In feverish work', Marc Friedmann will write in his journal. 'Cleaning up the filth of years,' Lydia will write in hers. At noon they take a break and eat sandwiches. At seven o'clock they hold a meeting in order to assess their activities. The Cleaning-up Committee has cleaned and tidied the house and decorated it with posters and banners supplied by the Political Studies Committee; in addition, having completed its tasks earlier than anticipated, the committee members have erected a new flagpole, the trunk of a eucalyptus tree. Mayer Guinzburg praises their accomplishment. The Food Committee has cooked a hot, reviving dinner, and when this is announced the Political Studies Committee postpones the reading of its report, seeing that it deals with complex issues, such as productivity, the control of power, and consciousness-raising. After dinner, they sit around a campfire and begin to sing war songs, which are followed by melancholy Yiddish songs. Finally, they lower the flag, Mayer Guinzburg delivers a brief speech on the tasks awaiting them, and then to bed. 20

# SCLIAR
Moacyr

## The Strange Nation of Rafael Mendes [A estranha nação de Rafael Mendes]

Scliar, a descendant of Russian-Jewish immigrants from the beginning of the century, has, since the early 1960s, led a dual career as a medical practitioner in Porto Alegre, capital of the southern state of Rio Grande do Sul, and as Brazil's leading Jewish fiction writer. This is his seventeenth book, originally published in 1983, and is his most explicit, if ironic, investigation into the history of the Jewish contribution to the making of Brazil — a still neglected subject shrouded in ignorance, despite evidence that the immigrant Portuguese population during colonial times was disproportionately Jewish (or converted New Christian) in its composition.

The idea of a crypto-judaic identity at work beneath the surface of Brazil's chequered evolution is the central theme of *The Strange Nation of Rafael Mendes*, which embraces a panoramic stretch of history and myth from Jonah's encounter in the belly of the whale, through the Diaspora to the Iberian peninsula and beyond to the South American New World.

In a characteristic blend of fact, speculation and fantasy, Scliar weaves his account of the Mendes dynasty, whose wanderings are driven in part by the dream of magical wealth, the Gold Tree, in part by the vision of a mythical country that bears more than a passing resemblance to a paradisiacal Brazil — 'a beautiful bay with waves lapping on the pure white sands of the beach, coconut trees, brightly coloured birds wheeling in flight, a gloriously blue sky, a country inhabited by friendly people (bronze-skinned men, women and children, their faces painted in gaudy colours, their long black hair adorned with feathers).'

Most of all, though, it is the perennial 'perplexity' of the Mendes nation, caught between the impulse to adventure, the wisdom of caution and restraint, and the dilemma of the Jewish condition, endlessly called to serve yet hounded by paranoia and suspicion. Such is the fate of the physician Maimonides, who discovers the cholera responsible for the illness of the Sultan Saladin, but is forced by the palace conspirators to collude in his death. Or of the Rafael Mendes, a descendant of New Christians, who foresees in a dream the execution of Tiradentes, the leader of an eighteenth-century revolutionary movement, but is disbelieved by those around him. Or of the doctor Rafael Mendes, appointed to a sinecure by the populist Vargas regime of the 1930s, and who becomes innocently embroiled in a scandal concerning an Indian land occupation, a mysterious epidemic, and a media campaign against the regime.

Something of an anti-epic, then, this unwritten history is a healthy antidote to other, more triumphalist accounts of nation-building, one in which the Mendes line plays a, by turns, unwilling, accidental or unheroic part. And when it finally does comes to light, it illuminates the life of its most recent protagonist against a background of renewed chaos and crisis, the Brazil of the mid 1970s, as the euphoria of the Economic Miracle is beginning to crumble. Only now is it revealed to an unsuspecting Rafael Mendes, the junior partner in a collapsing finance company, in the form of two notebooks left to him by his father, who had mysteriously disappeared to Spain at the time of the Civil War. Rafael reads the notebooks on the eve of his arrest for collusion in embezzlement, as he finds out that his wayward daughter has been having a secret affair with his best friend, the Jewish company director Boris Goldbaum ('Goldtree'), and that together they are plotting their escape to Paraguay.

One of the book's many ironies is that the pursuit of the mythical Gold Tree has led the last unwitting heir of the Mendes dynasty to an understanding of its foolish futility, in the shape of his failed business partner. With his life falling to pieces about him, surrounded by betrayal, the perplexed Rafael, one of a long line of perplexed Mendes, all at once discovers his own fantastic ancestry, his Jewishness no less, and is freed from 'the perplexity of generations' in order to confront his destiny, a wiser man. DT

He feels fine; now he feels fine. His head light, his forehead cool; fine. And thus he drifts off into drowsiness; and in this twilight between sleep and wakefulness, it seems to him that all of them are there, standing around the bed — Jonah and Habacuc, Maimonides and Rafael Mendes, all the ones named Rafael Mendes. In silence they look at him. Suddenly he realizes. All of them have the face he saw in the mirror a while ago; all of them are him, he is all of them. Now he understands the *Notebooks of the New Christians*; they are his father's legacy to him — Rafael is no longer beset by doubts. Instead of solutions, fantasies; instead of answers, imaginary possibilities. The perfect message from a perplexed individual, concludes Rafael — and then the figures begin to vanish, and he falls asleep. 296

# SCLIAR
Moacyr

## The Volunteers [Os Voluntários]

Moacyr Scliar is a native of Porto Alegre in the Southern 'Gaucho' state of Rio Grande do Sul. The city gets an affectionate salute in this book, particular the world of small shops and their keepers, here shown as very much an immigrant band of Portuguese, Polish-Jewish and Arab immigrants.

The central character of the novel is Benjamin, hopeless and heroic at the same time; a classic Diaspora Jewish figure. Part of his heroism is his struggle against his own real or imagined inadequacies. Like the somewhat parallel character of Meyer Guinzburg in Scliar's *One-Man Army* Benjamin is not really interested in inhabiting the limited possibilities of the reality that surrounds him; 'He was one of those people who yearn to live in a city they've never seen, to marry a woman they've never met, to read a book that has never been written'. Benjamin is a collision between Thurber's Walter Mitty, the henpecked suburban 'warrior' and that millennial Jewish figure the messianic dreamer. Benjamin draws breath only from the long-held vision of 'Jerusalem the Golden', the Jewish capital lost thousands of years ago but longed for every day. He is the embodiment of a kind of Jewish 'displacedness' that belies the success story of assimilation.

Dreaming of Jerusalem Benjamin rots away working in a clothes store but Scliar amuses himself by opening another clothes store next to Benjamin, whose proprietor is an Arab, a Palestinian, from…. Jerusalem. The two exiled proprietors of the Holy City face each other in the street…

Other characters here are equally tragi-comic, particularly perhaps the hooker Elvira, who has escaped from a stifling Italian agricultural colony to make a living in the only way she can on the Rua Voluntários and whose tawdry dream is to work in a high class brothel and not the run-down Maipu club on this sad street of immigrant shopkeepers, and Orígenes the ex-travelling salesman and would-be spiritual leader who represents a rather sad sect in Porto Alegre that echoes the Evangelicals currently setting the poor on fire in Brazil, by promising a kind of escape from generations of poverty and unease.

A work of sustained sympathetic humour that at the same time is about everyday despair, very Brazilian, very Jewish? RK

She disliked Rua Voluntarios: it had no class. She would rather work at a place like Mônica's, in the district of Cristal. *Mônica*, now that was a magical name, aristocratic even in the way it was pronounced. Elvira had never met Mônica. She imagined her as a tall, elegant lady, her blond hair carefully done, with diamond studded hoop earrings hanging from her earlobes, a genuine pearl necklace with an antique cameo adorning her lightly powdered bosom, an aura of French perfume enveloping her figure.

And what about Mônica's Place? Elvira visualized what it must be like: a mansion in the middle of a park. High walls, a wrought-iron game, armed guards. A driveway. A marquee. A doorman in livery opening the door. A lobby done in Roman marble. A receptionist stepping forward, eager to receive the hats, the fur-trimmed overcoats, the silver headed walking sticks (and rapiers?), the white silk scarves. Distinguished habitués: senators of the republic, well known professionals, financiers, representatives from the productive classes: captains of industry, big wheels of the business world, prosperous ranchers. Courteous, educated men. In a soft voice, they would chat with Mônica's girls (refined girls, many of them former normal school students, who wore silk and satin), as the girls languidly reclined on chaise tongues, puffing at their cigarettes with amber holders.

And the bedrooms. Ah, the bedrooms Elvira had heard wonders about those bedrooms, magnificently decorated (fur rugs, crystal chandeliers, hardwood furniture, fireplaces, bathrooms done in marble), each room in a different style. There was one in particular that roused her curiosity and envy. The Mirror Room, *all* of it — ceiling, walls, floor covered with crystal mirrors. At any given moment and from every possible angle, a couple could watch themselves making love. In the Mirror Room the lovers were, so to speak, suspended in an atmosphere of eyes and mouths, of thighs and buttocks... When a couple reached an orgasm in the Mirror Room, it was many couples that reached an orgasm. It would be impossible for a man to lose his erection in that room, impossible for a woman to remain frigid. That room was a temple to love. *Thanks to* — stated the advertising brochure of Mônica's Place — *the magic of the mirrors*.

Such magic Elvira had tried to reproduce in her room. She had placed mirrors, six of them, on the walls and ceiling. But the reflecting surface was too small. The largest mirror probably measured no more than twenty by fifty centimeters. They would capture half a boob; or three toes; or a hairy rump; or one nut. An atmosphere conducive to love? None whatsoever, not in her place. Her clients found the presence of all those mirrors odd (in order to comb one's hair, one mirror is enough), and never for a moment did they suspect that the mirrors were there as traps to capture the fleeting bird of love. Anyway, they weren't the type of men who would enjoy looking at themselves while screwing; they'd think it was something for men who couldn't get it up, or for fairies. Rua Voluntários will always remain Rua Voluntários, Elvira would say with a sigh, and the Maipu will always be the Maipu, and I'll always be in this shitty life. 52–53

## SOUZA
Márcio

## Mad Maria [Mad Maria]

Márcio Souza's action-packed novel revolves around the true events surrounding the construction of the infamous Madeira-Mamoré railroad on the Bolivian/Brazilian border in the early years of the twentieth century. Much of the international labour force brought to the remote Amazonian region to work on the railway perished from the effects of disease and the appalling conditions in which they were forced to work. With tragic irony, when the railroad was finally constructed it almost immediately became obsolete due to the collapse of the Brazilian rubber market.

Souza's narrative takes the reader back and forth between the construction of the railroad in the jungle, and the political and economic manoeuvrings in Rio de Janeiro which are behind the project. The novel features several historical figures involved in the affair, such as the Brazilian statesman Ruy Barbosa, and the North American industrialist Percival Farquhar, and gives the reader a vivid picture of the scramble by European and North American capitalists to exploit the potentially huge profits to be made in Brazil at the time.

Much of the novel centres on the savage infighting between the railway construction workers, many of whom have been hired under false pretences, and the cynical efforts of their exploitative employers to drive the project on. Excessive heat, torrential rain, and a multitude of ferocious insects all combine in a 'green hell' to reduce the railway's construction to a snail's pace. Yet as Souza demonstrates, the imported foreign workers are not the only victims of this venture, for local indigenous people are also savagely swept away, mere obstacles in the path of the locomotive, (the 'Mad Maria' of the title) which symbolizes 'progress'. Their plight is epitomised by one native Indian who, despite being horribly mutilated by railroad workers, throws in his lot with the Europeans, only to be subsequently reduced to the role of a circus attraction. Published in 1980, *Mad Maria* represents a heartfelt indictment of the author's concern over the destruction of the Amazonian environment and the human greed which allows it to take place. SS

The *civilized* were a difficult tribe to understand. From the top of a tall tree, invisible among the web of vines, he had seen everything and was frightened — not by the rifle shots but by the furious outbursts of hatred that the *whites* spewed forth echoing through the jungle. It also troubled him that, even though the light of life seemed to be extinguished so often among the *civilized*, they possessed no ceremony with which to treat their dead. It was as if only the very act of bringing death to themselves constituted a ceremony, and this he found difficult to accept. The *civilized* were powerful, nonetheless: they could build great constructions and they always had food, though they did no planting or hunting. Yet every day he felt obliged to withdraw in terror, because the intensity of hatred issuing from the *whites* was so painful to behold. He watched the *civilized* who had wrestled in the mud now get up and walk off in bitter silence. An older one of them, who was apparently their chief, came walking beneath him together with another, as the two were lost in conversation. What they were saying to each other was not difficult for him to understand; he had already managed to learn to speak many of their words. This, despite the fact that the *civilized* used a number of different languages; for he had observed that some among them did not even understand the language of their chief. 28–9

## VEIGA
José J.

### The Three Trials of Manirema [A Hora dos ruminantes]

A beautiful, flowing story of small-town life in a kind of Brazilian Wild West. As in Macondo, the town in Colombian Gabriel García Márquez's masterwork *One Hundred Years of Solitude,* Manirema is afflicted with various slightly humorous plagues; in Macondo it was butterflies and the loss of words so that the inhabitants had to write 'door' on the door and 'window' on the window while in Manirema there is a mass invasion, first of stray dogs, then of oxen that crowd the streets so thickly that children are sent as messengers to walk over their backs. Finally, and again reminiscent of García Márquez's book, there is the arrival of mysterious and threatening 'Outsiders' who leave as suddenly as they came.

Veiga has a delicious way with words as he creates the characters and conflicts of a small-town; the dispensing of folksy wisdom and the enacting of chronic feuds over the barrels of pork and chicken feed in the provisions store.

But amongst the young love and the Jabotica bushes is a modernist, sometimes Kafkaesque, edge too, that makes *Manirema* a punchy twentieth century work. RK

Strange dogs snoozing in doorways were treated with more consideration than children or old folks; people tip-toed to avoid disturbing them, some went as far as to enter their houses through the windows or the back door to keep from stepping on the animals. Many a tender meatball, fried in good fat, was served to them on the best china, the way an honoured guest would be treated. The whole town was virtually at the service of the animals; all other activity stopped or was postponed, relegated, forgotten. So long as it was a stranger, any flea-ridden, filthy, mangy dog could find someone to extol in it qualities that none could see but all confirmed. Being a strange dog in Manirema was a very advantageous thing. 57

# VERÍSSIMO
Érico

## Time and the Wind [O Continente]

This translation forms the first part of Veríssimo's huge trilogy *O Tempo e o Vento*, his hugely popular historical saga set in Rio Grande do Sul and spanning the period between 1745 and 1945. Over the course of its six hundred pages, *Time and the Wind* (1954) introduces the reader to a vast array of characters whose lives are played out in the shadow of historical events, from the days of Spanish and Portuguese rivalry over the control of the southernmost part of Brazil, until shortly after the declaration of the Republic in 1889. Running parallel to this human drama is the tale of the foundation and growth of the city of Santa Fé and its *sobrado* (mansion house) whose ownership symbolises the control of power in the region.

Veríssimo's swashbuckling narrative vividly recounts a history of family feuds that span generations. Jumping back and forth in time, and utilising interlocking plot lines which connect the various families together, the novel creates a vast panorama of war, rebellion, and fierce struggles over land, which is contrasted on a more intimate level with the eternal human cycle of birth, marriage and death. Born and raised in Rio Grande do Sul, Verissímo's work has been compared with that of Jorge Amado, in the sense that both writers set out to capture the essence of their native regions. In Veríssimo's case this encompasses the *gaúcho* tradition with its often fatalistic code of honour and obdurate resistance in the face of danger. For all its romanticism, *Time and the Wind* also dwells on themes such as the growth of European immigration to Brazil, the abolitionist movement and the rise of Republicanism. Veríssimo did not consider himself a 'writer's writer' and was the first to admit that his work was not innovative, yet his popularity within Brazil is an abiding testament to his skill as an old-fashioned storyteller. SS

The padre fell silent, folded the paper, and replaced it in his pocket.
'But why have I spoken of Garibaldi, who apparently has nothing to do with the day?' He made a brief pause, as if he expected some reply to

his rhetorical question. He raised his right arm, the index finger aimed. 'It is because the man who speaks to you is a priest, Italian by birth, who is beginning to be a Brazilian at heart; because in this same church today, seated among Brazilians, are Italian immigrants who nearly ten years ago arrived in this Province and founded in this very municipality of Santa Fé a colony which they called Garibaldina, in homage to the hero. And it is because those Italian colonists, just like the Germans of Nova Pomerânia, are working together with the Brazilians for the greatness of this municipality, this Province, this great nation. And in this land whose first conquerors bore names like Magalhães, Pereira, Fagundes, Xavier, Terra, live today men whose names are Bernardi, Nardini, Sorio, Conte, Bauermann, Schultz, Schneider, Schmidt, Kunz. And in this church I hope some day by the grace of God to unite in matrimony a Della Mea with a Pinto or a Spielvogel!' 541

ANTHOLOGY
Caistor, N.(Ed.)

## Faber Book of Contemporary Latin American Short Stories

This is an interesting, wide-ranging anthology of stories from all over Latin America, many by writers who are not translated in the UK (like Helio Vera) or only very poorly represented (like the marvellously witty Uruguayan writer Cristina Peri Rossi).

The two Brazilian writers represented here are João Ubaldo Ribeiro, who has three books available in the UK, and Moacyr Scliar, who has been published in the USA.

Ribeiro's short story 'Alaindelon de la Patrie' about a stud bull who hasn't quite got what it takes has him showing off his lightest touch; it's ironic, funny and ribald — a good introduction to its author. The Scliar story 'Peace and War' printed here is probably not enough to put this interesting Brazilian-Jewish writer on the map in the UK, but it's a start. It shows the writer in his humorous science-fiction mood, although in Brazil the lines between science fiction and straight fiction are not as constricting as in the English-speaking world.

As a fairly current sampler of Latin American writing this is a good and enjoyable collection. RK

The rooster sometimes seems to be conversing with its shadow or discussing elections or something when all of a sudden he flares up with great brilliance and begins pecking the chickens back and forth and puffing himself up in the direction of their tails, and thus he does all his work in something like five minutes, spark-like. The eggs that follow are brown, not white, fertile, not barren, and quite good for one's health, or else out come little chicks and all the chickens go on with their chickening as Our Lord wished. Thus the little lizard has two rods, one at the right, one at the left, so that any female lizard can be well provided whether she be left or right, and it should be said that the lizard only catches one lizardess at a time, not taking advantage of being able to serve two. For it is not a matter of vanity, it is a question of not wasting time, because if it is true that the lizard has many flies to eat, it is also true that there are many other creatures who want to eat the lizard, so he cannot afford to take it easy. 27 'Alaindelon De La Patrie' João Ubaldo Ribeiro

## ANTHOLOGY
Grossman, W. (Ed.)

### Modern Brazilian Short Stories

An anthology with sixteen Brazilian authors, first published in 1967 but still worth having today because created with such authority, professionalism and passion. Published by a US-based University press it may need a bit of tracking down in the UK.

There are here, as well as the great and the good already well-known in the Anglo-Saxon world, some authors considered highly in Brazil but not otherwise translated. An example is Marques Rebelo with his poignant story 'The Beautiful Rabbits', about childhood's insecurities and rivalries but with a sting of social critique in it too.

Mário de Andrade, the great man of Brazilian modernism famous for his extraordinary myth-novel *Macunaima*, is represented here with 'It can hurt plenty', an expert, moving story told, like Rebelo's, from a child's point of view. 'It can hurt plenty' is a small, casual masterpiece, as humane as Chekov, as socially aware as Orwell.

Other major stories in the collection are 'Metonymy' by Rachel de Queirós, written with great 'spring' and encapsulating very well the frequent ironic strain in Brazilian writing; 'The Thief' by Graciliano Ramos — like Rachel de Queirós another famous social novelist — is short with a sharp, filmic quality and finally there is Guimarães Rosa's *The Third Bank of the River,* a birthday present of a story, stunningly profound and resonant, a genuine touch of the spiritual. It would be worth getting the book for this story alone.

A genial part of this anthology is the provision of potted biographies at the end of each story; lives of Brazilian authors are often interesting in themselves. Altogether *Brazilian Short Stories* is an excellent starting point to explore Brazilian writing. RK

She was home. But could you really call it a home? It looked like one of those road huts where the mule drivers rest. Just about as dirty. Two things that looked vaguely like chairs. One table. One bed. On the floor

there was a mattress where the cockroaches lived. At night they came out and danced on the old lady's face. After all, where do all the insects of this world perform their tribal dances? On somebody's face, right?
13 Mário de Andrade 'It Can Hurt Plenty'

## ANTHOLOGY
Darlene J. Sadlier (Ed. and translator)

### One Hundred Years After Tomorrow: Brazilian Women's Fiction in the 20th Century

Darlene Sadlier's anthology does a great service to Brazilian writing: besides being an excellently translated and fascinatingly diverse collection of stories, it also opens an exciting window on the previously neglected field of women's fiction in Brazil. Twenty stories are included, ranging from 1907 to 1985, all published in English for the first time and many of them unavailable or unknown even in Brazil. Two factors provided the impetus for a groundbreaking collection such as this: the emergence from the 1970s of the women's movement in Brazil as part of the opposition to the military regime, and the special international reputation won by the work of Clarice Lispector since her 'discovery' by a number of feminist and other critics beyond the country's frontiers.

The contributors to the volume can be grouped roughly as follows: writers born in the second half of the nineteenth century and therefore overshadowed contemporaries of Machado de Assis, such as Carmen Dolores and Julia Lopes de Almeida, who were prize-winning authors in their own lifetimes but subsequently forgotten; more widely read, even popular names of the 1940s and 1950s, but who, apart from Rachel de Queiroz, likewise faded from public view and did not stay in print, such as Sra. Leandro Dupré and Emi Bulhões Carvalho da Fonseca; and the contemporary, post-1960s generation that includes some authors perhaps already familiar to non-Brazilian readers through foreign translations, such as Lispector, Lygia Fagundes Telles, Rachel de Queiroz and Nélida Piñon, but also others who still deserve greater recognition, such as Hilda Hilst, Marina Colasanti and Márcia Denser. Gender doesn't entirely dictate the subject-matter — Lia Correia Dutra's 'A Perfect World' peels away the anonymity of a tramp on the streets of Rio, for example, and Nélida Piñon's 'Near East' is a delicately intimate, mysterious encounter with the world of the exiled Turkish community. On the whole, though, the stories selected reflect the changing experience and consciousness of Brazilian women across the century.

Carmen Dolores' 'A Drama in the Countryside' and the extract from Sra. Leandro Dupré's *We Were Six* narrate from within the family life of the provincial middle classes. But many of the authors cross the class divide, from Rachel de Queiroz's drama of infant mortality in the drought-stricken North-east of the 1930s ('The Year Fifteen') and Tania Jamardo Faillace's portrait of a desperate single mother amidst the poverty of the contemporary big southern city; or Emi Bulhões Carvalho da Fonseca's shocking tale of the slave girl whose beautiful teeth are extracted to indulge the vanity of her young mistress 'In the Silence of the Big House', and Dinah Silveira de Queiroz's 'Jovita', about a kind of Brazilian Joan of Arc from the backlands who is cynically used to promote Brazil's war effort in the Triple Alliance conflict of the 1860s with Paraguay. Amongst the more recent explorations of female sexuality are Marina Colasanti's daring and provocative account of the dangerous interplay between adult male desire and preadolescent sexual self-awareness, under the reluctantly watchful, ambivalent eye of a concerned mother; and Márcia Denser's more hard-bitten, sardonic monologue of a jaded woman's cynical and fruitless search for a man one night in the city of São Paulo.

The reader's attention in this collection is also held by the variety of narrative and literary approaches employed, beyond the conventional social realism of the earlier authors. Lygia Fagundes Telles and Lya Luft explore in quite different ways the potential of the free-form monologue: Telles' middle-aged character (in 'Just a Saxophone') wistfully recalls the big, doomed love of her life, inevitably destroyed by obsessive narcissism, insecurity and dependency; while in the frighteningly surreal world of Luft's 'The Left Wing of the Angel', the narrator prepares to give birth to a monster conceived out of all the repressions of family life within a puritanical German immigrant community. There are techniques, too, derived from other, non-literary media, such as the cinematic "sequences" of scriptwriter Edla van Steen's 'The Sleeping Beauty (Script of a Useless Life)'; and the multi-voiced dialogues of Júlia Lopes de Almeida's 'He and She', spoken alternately by a husband and wife, Sônia Coutinho's 'Every Lana Turner Has Her Johnny Stompanato', with its interplay between authorial persona, character, icon and real-life individual, and the Joycean stream-of-consciousness of Hilda Hilst's 'Agda'. DT

I DIG. Constancy. Ten arm lengths deep. How many? Snails. Mud on my face. I have the look of someone half-buried. A gold that doesn't come. Nor the reflex. It'd be good to have a yellow light gilding the snails, the worms, my hand. It'd be good to recompose words, crisscross them, to say of the light, scintillating faceted filter, to say of the dark, just entrail, to say of the search what it is, the seeker and the sought, revealing the two sides, here you see yourself, here I am looking at you, the joyous orbit shattering fears, here when you were a little girl on top of the wall, hiding your face, the light parching your pupil, violet eyelid folded over, arm, forearm, end of the elbow pointing to the one taking a picture of you. Who was taking a picture of you? Mothermothermother beauty, the beret tilted to one side, curls in your hair covering the rosiness of your ears, mothermothermother beauty, let me touch your tender skin, or . . . fly, fly Medea, get away from me, travel across the spaces, cross all the bridges or go live under the water, let your father's reflex be just for me, *vere dignum et justus est, aequum et salutare*, let it be just for me.... because... because I would keep explaining it to you many nights or just screaming like the other one: woe, woe, Ah me, Ah me! Yes, now I'm knowing myself with this mud on my face, chewing me myself, burning wax consuming my body, consuming me and knowing me without nausea, throat wide-open, livid alchemist, go, Agda, deeper, without your knowing that your body is a sieve, miniscule orifices a thousand and one separating what is of worth, tasting, and letting the other trickle towards the well. Go, Agda, deeper, OH, I'm going, that tenuous body never again over me, oh, never again, life death expelled oh I was lucid, clean, my flesh was smooth, oh the joyous mysteries, the joy of myself, the great joy that is to sink into the old and yellow flesh in this mud and never again will anyone TOUCH ME, NEVER AGAIN NEVER AGAIN 154–55 Hilda Hilst 'Agda'

## ANTHOLOGY
Cristina Ferreira-Pinto (ed.)

### Urban Voices. Contemporary Short Stories from Brazil

There aren't nearly as many anthologies of Brazilian writing as this active and interesting literature requires, so this recent example — published in 2000 — should be something of an update, introducing many writers little-known in the English-speaking world.

Unfortunately, perhaps because of the pressure to be representative and inclusive etc. many of the stories chosen do not seem very strong. Marina Colasanti's 'Life Next Door' for example is hackneyed middlebrow 'avant-gardism' which has fallen way behind the 'garde'. More interesting is Tania Faillace's 'Great Neighbours', an elliptical look at death squads from the period of military rule in Brazil. In this piece here someone 'inconvenient' is done away with, quietly. No need to call the cops — they did it.

Hilda Hist, who the anthology's editor says is known as a 'difficult' writer tells us about 'Fine marble cries from an abandoned slut struggling to get her head in the armpit of God' while Sonia Coutinho's 'Last Summer in Copacabana' is about the relationships 'that have never worked out' of a pushing-forty media babe — her analyst can only tell her 'Everything's absurd, Helen'. The story moves in and out of the existential/elegiac and sophisticated: but is it? Another middlebrow meister Sérgio Sant'Anna provides 'German Submarine' from his book *O concerto de João Gilberto no Rio de Janeiro*.

Rubem Fonseca's 'Art of Walking in the streets of Rio de Janeiro' has some sparks of humour, as he takes a ramble with various oddballs and a prostitute: there's a failing evangelical pastor and the unmistakable whiff of cracked urban lives, which is Fonseca's beat. He's on better than average form here while Regina Célia Colônia-Willner's 'Copacabana from 5 to 7' is almost as pretentious as her name... Caio Fernando Abreu's more-than-wistful 1983 story 'The Sailor' advertises his romantic sensitivity but in a far less focussed way than in his better later work.

Edgard Telles Ribeiro's 'Chocolate Mousse' is frothy but tasty and Moacyr Scliar, the much-translated Brazilian-Jewish writer, appears here with a very light-hearted piece 'Oral Passions' about a gorgeous dentist and her lovestruck patient; 'God, she was beautiful, the most beautiful woman I'd ever seen, a brunette with green eyes. Her lips were fleshy like the pulp of a fruit. She had a perfect body... God, how could such a beautiful woman have become a dentist?'

Márcia Denser, born in 1949, is ten years younger than many of the other writers here and writes 'contos eróticos femininos' or erotic stories for women. The quote from her story given here is not erotic, about an mother fearful of ageing, but it is amusing. Her 'The Last Tango in Jacobinha' takes a well-worn erotic theme, 'the princess and the pauper', a 'rough trade' saga, but its crescendo is of self-inflicted violence rather than sexual climax. Maybe she is an author we should know more about.

We get a wonderfully acidic account of a city of the interior in 'Canguçu' by Dinorath do Valle — '...the town is a pretentious thing, it thinks it's alive, it already has just about everything it needs to be unhappy but it's pushing for more: paved streets and bare feet, full markets and empty men, mendicants and labour syndicates, dry faucets and closed wells, there's even a census for the dogs.' (196)

Another and much better-known city of the interior; Brasilia, has its story told in Luis Fernando Emediato's 'The Other Side of Paradise' but, unusually, from the point of view of its builders who lived in a conveniently out of sight shantytown. Emediato actually provides a compressed social history of Brasilia and of Brazil too, its best and worst moments and a story too of moral and spiritual resistance to disillusionment and corruption.

Silviano Santiago is a professor of Literature who writes (is that necessarily a bad sign? Think Saul Bellow not Hélène Cixous) and is a tremendously fluent writer but is there anything beneath the shiny surface of his prose? His piece here 'You Don't Know What Love Is/ Muezzin' contributes however a spectacularly awful dish to the repertoire of literary recipes and is reproduced below — but please don't try it at home.

Although this anthology represents something of a tour of writers active since the 1970s in Brazil maybe six out of twenty stories really register on the literary 'qualitometer' — the editor seems to have mislaid her critical faculties when she entered the literature faculty. RK

I remember her at home, almost always sprawled out on a red velvet sofa, her sigh, quickly swallowed up by the inscrutable expression of a bored she-wolf, calm and motionless like the surface of a swamp, or that monotonous, unmodulating voice that prattled on and on, the sudden swishing of a negligee disappearing through a door, dragging the interminable: telephone cord (because the conversations with her friends are also interminable and always the same, labyrinthine), a sort of Ariadne's thread that gradually winds around Chinese vases, statuettes, antique chests, bronze pedestals, Chippendale tables, disappearing under the drapes, under the heavy, perpetually closed curtains that filter a fine mist of hysterical particles, creating that gritty atmosphere of red and hot ashes of Pharaonic tombs, while she weaves and unweaves the same mindless yarn, endlessly returning to the sofa, to sighing and to boredom.

Through her obsession with preserving her youth and stopping time, she ended up mummifying herself. She and her withered camellias, her purple taffeta dresses, her trinkets buried at the bottom of the closet full of mirrors, in the depth of mirrors. 179-80 Márcia Denser 'The Last Tango in Jacobinha'

The appetizer is already chosen. *Champignons farcis au thon.* You open a can of Italian, white tuna. You dump the can's contents into a bowl, add a half a tablespoon of mayonnaise, a few drops of Tabasco. The tuna already has a lot of salt Your right thumb pulverises dried leaves of *fines herbes* in the palm of your left hand. You sprinkle the dark green powder over the bowl. You mix the ingredients until they turn into a paste. You cover the bowl with plastic wrap. You place it next to the wrapped mushrooms.

From the bottom drawer of the refrigerator, you take out a

plastic bag with four leaves of endive. You turn on the oven. From the top drawer, you take out the ham wrapped in aluminium foil. You choose the four most consistent slices. After washing them, you roll each leaf of endive with a slice of ham, skewering a toothpick into the little roll so it won't come apart. You pick up a package of *Knorr's* white sauce. In a saucepan, you prepare the white sauce, slowly adding milk mixed with water. You look for a rectangular glass baking dish in the cupboard. The smallest. You arrange the four rolls in the dish and cover them with the white sauce. You put the dish in the oven to brown.

While the oven does its job, you grab a frying pan. You turn on the gas burner. You let the butter melt and add the mushrooms upside down. Low heat. You cover the frying pan. Five minutes later, you take out the lightly cooked mushrooms and arrange them on a plate, still upside down and you stuff them wit the tuna and mayonnaise mixture. 237 Silviano Santiago 'You Don't Know What Love Is/Muezzin'

# Contributors

**Ray Keenoy**
is founder and editor of the Babel Guides series
**David Treece**
is a translator and Director of the Centre for the Study of Brazilian Culture and Society at King's College London
**David Brookshaw**
is Professor of Lusophone Studies at the University of Bristol
**Aviva Cohen** is a young actress and writer who has studied literature at universities in Canada and France.
**Marina Coriolano-Lykourezos**
works in publishing and cinema in Greece
**Maria Amelia Dalsenter**
works in publishing in Brazil
**Stephanie Dennison**
lectures at the University of Leeds
**Angela Dierks**
works in higher education in the United Kingdom
**John Gledson**
is Professor of Brazilian Literature at the University of Liverpool
**Robert Howes**
is a librarian at the University of Sussex
**Tom MacCarthy**
is an author
**Nancy Naro**
lectures at King's College London
**Giovanni Pontiero (1932-96)**
was the principal translator into English of the work of Clarice Lispector, José Saramago and many other Lusophone writers
**Siobhan Smith**
is studying for a PhD
**Sean Stroud**
is a postgraduate researcher at King's College London
**Claire Williams**
lectures at the University of Liverpool

# Database of Brazilian Fiction in Translation

This database lists literature – novels, short story collections, anthologies, poetry and drama – translated into English. For convenience Anthologies are generally listed under 'Anthology'.

Record details;

Author surname
Author first name
English title
Original title
Translator
Year published in Portuguese
Year published in English
US or other Publisher
Pages
UK Publisher

ABREU
Caio Fernando
Dragons
*Os Dragões não conhecem o Paraíso*
1988
Treece, David
Boulevard: Oxford
1990
pb
148

ABREU
Caio Fernando
Whatever happened to Dulce Veiga?: a B-novel
*Onde andará Dulce Veiga?*
Adria Frizzi
Universiy of Texas
2001
192
pb

ADONIAS FILHO
Aguiar
Memories of Lazarus
*Memorias de Lazaro*
Ellison, Fred P.
Texas UP
1952

ADONIAS FILHO
Aguiar
Memories of Lazarus
*Memorias de Lazaro*
Ellison, Fred P.
Texas UP
1969
170

ALBUES
Tereza
Pedra Canga
Landers, Clifford E.
Green Integer Series Paperback 7
2000
140

ALENCAR
Jose Martiniano
Iracema, the Honey-lips, a legend of BRazil
*Iracema*
1865
Landers, Clifford E.
OUP NY
2000
148
OUP, Oxford
2000
148

ALENCAR
Jose Martiniano
Iracema, the Honey-lips, a legend of Brazil
*Iracema*
1865
Burton, Sir Richard & Isabel
Fertig
1976

ALENCAR
Jose Martiniano
Iracema, the Honey-lips, a legend of Brazil
*Iracema*
1865
Burton, Sir Richard & Isabel
Bickers & Son:London
1886

ALENCAR
Jose Martiniano
Senhora: Profile of a woman
*Senhora*
1875
Edinger, Catarina Feldmann
Texas UP: Austin
1994
hb
198

ALENCAR
Jose Martiniano
Senhora: Profile of a woman
*Senhora*
1875
Edinger, Catarina Feldmann
Texas UP: Austin
1994
hb
198

ALMEIDA
José Américo de
Trash, a novel
*Bagaceira, A*
1928
Scott-Buccleuch, R.L.
Owen
1978
160

ALMEIDA
Manuel Antonio De
Memoirs of a Militia Sergeant : A Novel
1852
Ronald W. Sousa
OUP
2000
224

AMADO
Jorge
Captains of the Sand
*Capitães da Areia*
1937
Rabassa, Gregory
Avon
1988
pb
248

AMADO
Jorge
Dona Flor and Her Two Husbands
*Dona Flor e seus dois maridos*
1966
Onis, Harriet de
Knopf
1969
hb
553

AMADO
Jorge
Dona Flor and Her Two Husbands
*Dona Flor e seus dois maridos*
1966
Onis, Harriet de
Serpent's Tail
1986
pb
553

AMADO
Jorge
Dona Flor and Her Two Husbands
*Dona Flor e seus dois maridos*
1966
Onis, Harriet de
Weidenfeld
1969
hb
553

AMADO
Jorge
Gabriela, Clove and Cinnamon
*Gabriela, cravo e canela*
1958
Taylor, James L. & Grossman, W.L.
Knopf
1962

AMADO
Jorge
Gabriela, Clove and

153

Cinnamon
*Gabriela, cravo e canela*
1958
Taylor, James L. & Grossman, W.L.
Fawcett, Greenwich, Conn
1964
400

AMADO
Jorge
Gabriela, Clove and Cinnamon
*Gabriela, cravo e canela*
1958
Taylor, James L. & Grossman, W.L.
Souvenir
1983
hb

AMADO
Jorge
Gabriela, Clove and Cinnamon
*Gabriela, cravo e canela*
1958
Taylor, James L. & Grossman, W.L.
Abacus
1984
pb

AMADO
Jorge
Gabriela, Clove and Cinnamon
*Gabriela, cravo e canela*
1958
Taylor, James L. & Grossman, W.L.
Chatto
1963
pb
425

AMADO
Jorge
Golden Harvest, The
*São Jorge dos Ilhéus*
1944
Landers, Clifford E.
Avon
1992
pb
359

AMADO
Jorge
Home is the Sailor
*Completa Verdade sobre as discutidas avent... Com, V.M. de Aragão*
1961
Onis, Harriet de

Knopf, New York
1964
hb
298

AMADO
Jorge
Home is the Sailor
*Completa Verdade sobre as discutidas aventuras do Comandante Vasco Moscoso de Aragão, capitão de longo curso*
1961
Onis, Harriet de
Harvill
1990
pb
256

AMADO
Jorge
Home is the Sailor
*Completa Verdade sobre... Com, V.M. de Aragão*
1961
Onis, Harriet de
Chatto
1964
hb
295

AMADO
Jorge
Home is the Sailor
*Completa Verdade sobre as discutidas avent... Com, V.M. de Aragão*
1961
Onis, Harriet de
Avon NY
1979
pb
255

AMADO
Jorge
Jubiabá
*Jubiabá*
1935
Neves, Margaret A.
Avon
1984
294

AMADO
Jorge
Pen, Sword, Camisole
*Farda, Fardão, Camisola de Dormir*
1979

Lane, Helen
Avon
1986
pb

AMADO
Jorge
Pen, Sword, Camisole
*Farda, Fardão, Camisola de Dormir*
1979
Lane, Helen
Godlne
1985
hb

AMADO
Jorge
Pen, Sword, Camisole
*Farda, Fardão, Camisola de Dormir*
1979
Lane, Helen
Avon
1986
pb

AMADO
Jorge
Sea of Death
*Mar Morto*
1936
Rabassa, Gregory
Avon
1984
273

AMADO
Jorge
Shepherds of the Night
*Pastores da noite, Os*
1966
Onis, Harriet de
Knopf
1967
264

AMADO
Jorge
Shepherds of the Night
*Pastores da noite, Os*
1966
Onis, Harriet de
Harvill
1989
pb
384

AMADO
Jorge
Showdown
*Tocaia Grande*
1985

AMADO
Jorge
Slums
*Suor*
Rabassa, Gregory
Bantam
1988
422

AMADO
Jorge
Slums
*Suor*
New Americas: NY
1937

AMADO
Jorge
Swallow and the Tom Cat,
The. A love story.
*Gato Malhado e a
Andoninho Sinhá*
Merollo, Barbara Shelby
Delacorte P: NY
96

AMADO
Jorge
Tent of Miracles
*Tenda dos milagres*
Shelby, Barbara
Knopf
1971
hb
392

AMADO
Jorge
Tent of Miracles
*Tenda dos milagres*
Shelby, Barbara
Harvill
1989
pb
392

AMADO
Jorge
Teresa Batista: Home from
the Wars
*Teresa Batista, cansada de
guerra*
Merello, Barbara Shelby
Avon
1988
pb
576

AMADO
Jorge
Teresa Batista: Home from
the Wars
*Teresa Batista, cansada de
guerra*
Merello, Barbara Shelby

AMADO
Jorge
Teresa Batista: Home from
the Wars
*Teresa Batista, cansada de
guerra*
Merello, Barbara Shelby
Random House
1975
hb
576

AMADO
Jorge
Teresa Batista: Home from
the Wars
*Teresa Batista, cansada de
guerra*
Merello, Barbara Shelby
Souvenir P (Condor books)
1982
hb
551

AMADO
Jorge
Teresa Batista: Home from
the Wars
*Teresa Batista, cansada de
guerra*
Merello, Barbara Shelby
Abacus
1983
pb
576

AMADO
Jorge
Tieta the Goat Girl
*Tieta do Agreste*
1977
Merollo, Barbara Shelby
Knopf
1979
671

AMADO
Jorge
Tieta the Goat Girl
*Tieta do Agreste*
1977
Merollo, Barbara Shelby
Souvenir
1981
hb
671

AMADO
Jorge
Tieta the Goat Girl
*Tieta do Agreste*
1977
Merollo, Barbara Shelby
Abacus
1982
pb
671

AMADO
Jorge

Two Deaths of Quincas
Wateryell; A Tall Tale.
*A morte e a morte de
Quincas Berro d'agua*
Shelby, Barbara
Avon
1965
pb
112

AMADO
Jorge
Two Deaths of Quincas
Wateryell; A Tall Tale.
*A morte e a morte de
Quincas Berro d'agua*
Shelby, Barbara
Knopf
1965
97

AMADO
Jorge
Violent Land
*Terras do sem-fim*
1942
Putnam, Samuel
Knopf
1965
336

AMADO
Jorge
Violent Land
*Terras do sem-fim*
1942
Putnam, Samuel
Harvill
1989
pb
320

AMADO
Jorge
War of the Saints
*Sumiço da Santa, O*
Rabassa, G
Serpent's Tail
1994
pb
357

AMADO
Jorge
War of the Saints
*Sumiço da Santa, O*
Rabassa, G
Bantam: NY
1993
357
Serpent's Tail
1994

ANDRADE
Mário de
Fraulein
*Amar, verbo intransitivo*
1927
Hollingworth, Margaret Richardson
MacCauly, New York
1933

ANDRADE
Mário de
Hallucinated City
*Pauliceia desvairada*
1922
Tomlins, Jack E.
Vanderbilt UP
1969

ANDRADE
Mário de
Macunaima
*Macunaima, o herói sem nenhum caráter*
1928
Goodland, E.A.
Quartet
1988
hb
170

ANDRADE
Mário de
Macunaima
*Macunaima, o herói sem nenhum caráter*
1928
Goodland, E.A.
Quartet
1988
pb
170

ANDRADE
Mário de
Macunaíma
*Macunaíma, o herói sem nenhum caráter*
1928
Goodland, E.A.
Random House
1984
168

ANDRADE
Oswald de
Sentimental Memoirs of John Seaborne, The
*Memórias sentimentais de João Miramar*
1923
Nefertiti Head Press: Austin
1979

ANDRADE
Oswald de
Seraphim Grosse Pointe
*Serafim Ponte Grande*
1933
Jackson, Kenneth & Bork, Albert
New Latin Quarter Editions/ Nefertiti Head P.: Austin
1979
131

ANGELO
Ivan
Celebration, A
*Festa, A*
Thomas Colchie
Avon
1982
223

ANGELO
Ivan
Tower of Glass, The
*Casa de vidro: cinco historias do Brasil*
Watson, Ellen
Avon
1986

ANJOS, Cyro dos
Cyro dos
Diary of a Civil Servant
*Amanuense Belmiro, O*
1937
Brakel, Arthur
Fairleigh Dickinson UP: Toronto
1986
179

ANTHOLOGY
Scents of Wood and Silence: short stories by Latin American Women Writers
Latin American Literary Review P
1991
218

ANTHOLOGY (Albert Manguel ed.)
Other Fires: Short Fiction by Latin American Women
Potter: NY
1986
222

ANTHOLOGY (Albert Manguel ed.)
Other Fires: Short Fiction by Latin American Women
Pan
1986
pb
222

ANTHOLOGY (Bishop, E. & Brasil, E. eds)
Anthology of 20th Century Brazilian Literature, An
Wesleyan UP: Middletown
1972

ANTHOLOGY (Blackburn P. et al. (tr.s))
Prize Stories from Latin America
Various
Doubleday: NY
1964

ANTHOLOGY (Caistor Nick Ed.)
Contemporary Latin American Short Stories, Faber Book of
Various
Faber
1989
hb
188

ANTHOLOGY (Cohen J.M.)
Latin American Writing Today
Various
Penguin
1967
pb
267

ANTHOLOGY (Cristina Ferreira Pinto ed.)
Urban Voices: Contemporary Short Stories from Brazil
University Press of America
2000
288

ANTHOLOGY (Darlen Joy Sadlier ed.)
One hundred years after tomorrow: Brazilian women's fiction in the 20th century
Darlen Joy Sadlier
Indiana Univ. P: Bloomington, IN
1992
241

ANTHOLOGY (Donald

Yates ed.)
Latin Blood: the best crime & detective stories of South America
Herder: NY
1972

ANTHOLOGY (Donoso, Jose, Henkin, William ed.s)
Triquarterly Anthology of Contemporary Latin American Literature
Dutton: NY
1969

ANTHOLOGY (Edla van Steen ed.)
Love stories, a Brazilian collection
*Papel do amor*
George, David Sanderson
Gráfica Editora: São Paulo
1978
198

ANTHOLOGY (Flores, Angel & Poore, Dudley, Ed.s)
Fiesta in November: stories from Latin America
Various
Houghton Mifflin: Boston
1942

ANTHOLOGY (Goldberg, Isaac ed.)
Brazilian Tales
Int'l Pocket Library: Boston
1965
96

ANTHOLOGY (Goldberg, Isaac ed.)
Brazilian Tales
Brandon Publishers (US)
1963 (1924
149

ANTHOLOGY (Grossman, William ed.)
Modern Brazilian Short Stories
Grossman, William
California UP: Berkeley
1967
pb
167

ANTHOLOGY (Grossman, William ed.)
Modern Brazilian Short Stories
Grossman, William
California UP: Berkeley
1974
pb

ANTHOLOGY (Jose S. de G. Coelho Pinto ed.)
New Brazilian Short Stories/ Contistas brasileiros
Horton, Rod W.
Revista Branca: Rio de Janeiro
1957
238

ANTHOLOGY (Kalechofsky, Robert ed.)
Echad, an Anthology of Latin American Jewish Writings
Micah Publications: Marblehead, MA.
1980
282

ANTHOLOGY (Leyland, Winston ed.)
Now the Volcano: an anthology of Latin American Gay Writings
Erskine Lane et al
Gay Sunshine P: San Francisco, CA
287

ANTHOLOGY (Marjorie Agosin ed.)
Landscapes of a New Land: fiction by Latin American Women
White Pine P: Buffalo, NY
1989
194

ANTHOLOGY (Miriam Alves & Carolyn Richardson ed.s)
Finally — us: contemporary Black Brazilian women writers (bi-lingual)
*Enfim — nos: escritoras negras brasileiras contemporâneas*
Three Continents P: Colorado Springs, CO
1995
258

ANTHOLOGY (Pat McNees Mancini ed.)
Contemporary Latin American Short Stories
Fawcett: Greenwich, Conn.
1974

ANTHOLOGY (Simpson, Amelia ed.)
New Tales of mystery and crime from Latin America
Amelia S. Simpson
Fairleigh Dickinson
161

ANTHOLOGY (Winston Leyland ed.)
My deep dark pain is love: a collection of Latin American gay fiction
Gay Sunshine P: San Frabncisco
383

ANTHOLOGY (ed. Margarite Fernández Olmos et al)
Pleasure in the word: erotic writings by Latin American women
White Pine P: Fredonia, NY
1993
284

ANTHOLOGY
ArturoTorres-Riosecco ed.)
Short stories of Latin America
Nelken, Z. & Torres-Riosecco, A.
Las Americas: NY
1963

ARANHA
José Pereira da Graça
Canaã
*Canaa*
1902
Lorente, Joaquim Mariano
Four Seas: Boston
1920

ARANHA
José Pereira da Graça
Canaã
*Canaa*
1902
Lorente, Joaquim Mariano
Allen & Unwin
1921

AZEVEDO
Aluizio de

157

Brazilian Tenement, A
Brown, Harry W,
Fertig Inc.
1977
320

AZEVEDO
Aluizio de
Brazilian Tenement, A
*Cortiço, O*
1890
Brown, Harry R.
Fertig: NY
1976

AZEVEDO
Aluizio de
Brazilian Tenement, A
*Cortiço, O*
1890
Brown, Harry R.
Cassell: London
1928

AZEVEDO
Aluizio de
Mulatto
*Mulato, O*
Murray, Graeme MacNicoll
Fairleigh Dickinson UP:Toronto
1990
298

AZEVEDO
Aluizio de
Mulatto
*Mulato, O*
1881
Murray, Graeme MacNicoll
Associated UP: London
1990
298

AZEVEDO
Aluizio de
Slum, The
*Cortiço, O*
1890
OUP: Oxford
2000
256

BARROSO
Gustavo
Mapirunga
*Mapirunga*
Cunningham-Grahame, RB
Heinemann
1924
40

BRANDAO
Ignacio de Loyola
Zero
*Zero*
1975
Watson, Ellen
Avon
1984
pb

BUARQUE DE HOLLANDA
Chico
Benjamin
*Benjamin*
Landers, Clifford E.
Bloomsbury
1997
150

BUARQUE DE HOLLANDA
Chico
Benjamin
*Benjamin*
Landers, Clifford E.
Bloomsbury
1998
196

BUARQUE DE HOLLANDA
Chico
Turbulence
*Estorvo*
1991
Peter Bush
Bloomsbury
1992
224

BUARQUE DE HOLLANDA
Chico
Turbulence
*Estorvo*
1991
Peter Bush
Pantheon Books: NY
1992
164
Bloomsbury
1992
224

BUARQUE DE HOLLANDA
Chico
Turbulence
*Estorvo*
1991
Peter Bush
Bloomsbury
1997

CALLADO
Antonio
Don Juan's Bar
*Bar Don Juan*
1971
Shelby, Barbara
Knopf: NY
1972
271

CALLADO
Antonio
Quarup
*Quarup*
1967
Shelby, Barbara
Knopf: NY
1970

CAMINHA
Adolfo
Bom-Crioulo: the Black man and the cabin boy
*Bom-Crioulo*
E.A.Lacey
Gay Sunshine P.:San Francisco, CA
141

CARNEIRO
Cecilio
Bonfire, The
*Fogueira, A*
1939
Poore, Dudley
Greenwood P: Westport, Conn.
1972
hb
334

CASTRO
Ferreira de
Jungle; A Tale of the Amazon Rubbertappers
*A Selva*
Charles Duff
Viking: NY, NY
1935
351

CASTRO
Josué de
Of Men and Crabs
*Homens e caranguejos*
Susan Hertelendy
Vanguard P: NY
1970
190

COELHO
Paulo
Alchemist, The

*Alquimista, O*
Clarke, Alan R.
Harper San Francisco
1993
177

**COELHO**
Paulo
Alchemist, The
*Alquimista, O*
Clarke, Alan R.
Harper San Francisco
1993
pb
177

**COELHO**
Paulo
Alchemist, The
*Alquimista, O*
Clarke, Alan R.
Hall: Thorndike ME (Large Print)
207
Large Print
hb

**COELHO**
Paulo
Alchemist, The
*Alquimista, O*
Clarke, Alan R.
Thorsons London
1995
hb
177

**COELHO**
Paulo
By the river Piedra I sat down and wept
*Na margem do rio Piedra eu sentei e chorei*
Clarke, Alan R.
Harper: San Francisco
1994
210
Thorsons London
1997
224

**COELHO**
Paulo
Devil and Miss Prym, The
*O Demonio e a Srta. Prym*
HarperCollins
2001

**COELHO**
Paulo
Diary of a Magus
*Diário de um mago, O*
Clarke, Alan R.
Harper San Francisco
1992
226

**COELHO**
Paulo
Fifth Mountain, The
*Quinta montanha*
Landers, Clifford E.
HarperCollins: London
1998
245

**COELHO**
Paulo
Illustrated Alchemist, The
*Alquimista, O*
Clarke, Alan R.
HarperCollins
1998
hb
198

**COELHO**
Paulo
Paulo Coelho Collection, The
Thorsons
1997
pb

**COELHO**
Paulo
Pilgrimage, The
*Diário de um mago*
Thorsons
1997
pb
240

**COELHO**
Paulo
Valkyries, The
*Valkírias*
Thorsons
1996
pb
245

**COELHO**
Paulo
Veronika decides to die
*Veronika decide morrer*
Harper Perennial
2001
224
HarperCollins
2001

**CORÇÃO**
Gustavo
My neighbour as myself
*Descoberta do outro, A*
1944
Wilson, Clotilde
Longmans Green: London
1957

**CORÇÃO**
Gustavo
Who If I Cry Out?
*Licoes de Abismo*
Wilson, Clotilde
Texas UP: Austin
1967
217

**COUTINHO**
Edilberto
Bye, Bye Soccer
*Maracanã, Adeus*
Loria, W & Bratcher, J
Host: Austin, Tx.
1994
136

**CUNHA**
Euclydes da
Rebellion In The Backlands
*Os sertões*
Samuel Putnam
Chicago, U. of Chicago
1959
532

**CUNHA**
Euclydes da
Rebellion in the Backlands
*Sertões, Os*
Putnam, Samuel
Gollancz
1947
347

**CUNHA**
Euclydes da
Rebellion in the Backlands
*Sertões, Os*
Putnam, Samuel
Texas UP: Austin

**CUNHA**
Helena Parente
Woman Between Mirrors
*Mulher no Espelho*
Ellison, F.P. & Lindstrom, N.
Texas UP
132

**CUNHA**
Helena Parente
Woman Between Mirrors.
*Mulher no Espelho*
Ellison, F.P. & Lindstrom, N.
Polygon
1990

159

CÉSAR
Ana Cristina
Intimate Diary
*various*
David Treece
Boulevatrd: dist. SBS, Seattle
1997
128
Boulevard: Oxford
1997
128

DOURADO
Autran
Bells of Agony
*Sinos da agonia, Os*
1974
Parker, John
Owen
1988
hb
224

DOURADO
Autran
Hidden Life, A
*Vida em Segredo, Uma*
1964
Miller, Edgar (Jnr.)
Knopf: NY
1969
150

DOURADO
Autran
Pattern for a Tapestry
*Risco do bordado, O*
1970
Parker, John
Owen
1984
hb
169

DOURADO
Autran
Pattern for a Tapestry
*Risco do bordado, O*
1970
Parker, John
Penguin
1986
pb
169

DOURADO
Autran
Taxi, or Poem of love in transit
*Taxi ou poema do amor passageiro*
Perrone, Charles A.
Garland: NY
1992

DOURADO
Autran
Voices of the Dead
*Ópera dos mortos*
Parker, John
Taplinger: NY
1980
hb
248

DOURADO
Autran
Voices of the Dead
*Ópera dos mortos*
1967
Parker, John
Owen
1980
hb
248

DOURADO
Autran
Voices of the Dead
*Ópera dos mortos*
1967
Parker, John
Zenith: Feltham
1983
hb
248

FELINTO
Marilene
Women of Tijucopapo, The
*Mulheres de Tijucopapo*
1982
Matthews, Irene
Nebraska UP
1994
pb
132

FELINTO
Marilene
Women of Tijucopapo, The
*Mulheres de Tijucopapo*
1982
Matthews, Irene
Nebraska UP
1994
hb
132

FELINTO
Marilene
Women of Tijucopapo, The
*Mulheres de Tijucopapo*
1982
Matthews, Irene
Nebraska UP:dist AUPG
1994
hb
132

FELINTO
Marilene
Women of Tijucopapo, The
*Mulheres de Tijucopapo*
1982
Matthews, Irene
Nebraska UP:dist AUPG
1994
pb
132

FONSECA
Rubem
Bufo & Spallanzani
*Bufo & Spallanzani*
Landers, Clifford E.
Dutton: NY
1989

FONSECA
Rubem
High Art
*Grande Arte, A*
1983
Watson, Ellen
Carroll & Graf
1987
pb
345

FONSECA
Rubem
High Art
*Grande Arte, A*
1983
Watson, Ellen
Collins
1987
pb
345

FONSECA
Rubem
High Art
*Grande Arte, A*
1983
Watson, Ellen
Harper: NY
1986
pb
345

FONSECA
Rubem
Lost Manuscript, The
*Vastas emoções e*

*pensamentos imperfeitos*
1988
Landers, Clifford E.
Bloomsbury
1997
256

**FRANÇA**
Oswaldo
Beneath the Waters
*No fundo dos águas*
Margaret A. Neves
Ballantine: NY
1990
165

**FRANÇA**
Oswaldo
Long Haul, The
*Jorge, um brasileiro*
Thomas Colchie
Dutton NY
1980
184

**FRANÇA**
Oswaldo
Man in the Monkey Suit, The
*Homem do macacão, O*
Gregory Rabassa
Ballantinr:NY
1986
102

**FREYRE**
Gilberto
Mother and Son. A Brazilian Tale
*Dona Sinha e o filho padre*
Barbara Shelby
Knopf
1967
232

**GALVÃO**
Patrícia (Pagu)
Industrial Park
*Parque Industrial*
1933
Jackson, Eliz. & K. David
Nebraska UP
1993
153
Nebraska UP
1993
hb
153

**GALVÃO**
Patrícia (Pagu)
Industrial Park
*Parque Industrial*
1933

Jackson, Eliz. & K. David
Nebraska UP
1993
pb
153

**GAMA**
Jose Basilio de
Uruguay, The
*Uraguai, O*
1769
Burton, Richard
California UP: Berkeley
1983
270

**GOMES**
Dias
Journey to Bahia
*O pagador de promessas*
Brazilian American Cultural Institute, Washington DC
1964
79

**GOMES**
Paulo Emilio Salles
P.'s Three Women
*Três mulheres de três PPPês*
1977
Neves, Margaret Abigail
Avon
1984

**GUIMARÃES ROSA**
João
Devil to pay in the backlands, The
*Grande Sertao: veredas*
1956
Taylor, J.L. & de Onis, Harriet
Knopf
1963

**GUIMARÃES ROSA**
João
Jaguar, The. A New Selection and translation of Guimaraes Rosa's greatest stories.
*Primeiras histórias and Estas estórias (selection)*
David Treece
Boulevard: dist ISBS Seattle
2001
Boulevard: Oxford
2001

**GUIMARÃES ROSA**
João

Sagarana
*Sagarana*
1946
Onis, Harriet de
Knopf
1963,1966
303

**GUIMARÃES ROSA**
João
Third bank of the river and other stories, The
*Primeiras estorias*
1962
Shelby, Barbara
Knopf
1968
238

**HATOUM**
Milton
Tree of the seventh heaven
*Relato de um certo oriente*
Ellen Watson
Atheneum: NY
1994
210

**IVO**
Lêdo
Snakes' Nest: or, a tale badly told
*Ninho de cobras*
Krapohl, Ken
New Directions NY
1981
136
Owen
1989
hb
136

**LIMA BARRETO**
Afonso Henriques Lima
Claro dos Anjos
*Claro dos Anjos*
Fitz, E
Yale UP: New Haven
1977

**LIMA BARRETO**
Afonso Henriques
Patriot, The
*Triste Fim de Policarpo Quaresma*
1915
Buccleuch, Robert Scott
Rex Collings
1978
hb
216

LINS

Osman
Avalovara
*Avalovara*
1973
Rabassa, Gregory
Knopf: NY
1980
331

LINS
Osman
Avalovara
*Avalovara*
1973
Rabassa, Gregory
Texas UP
1990

LINS
Osman
Nine, Novena
*Nove, novena*
1966
Frizzi, A
Sun & Moon: Los Angeles, CA
1995
276
Sun & Moon: dist. Password
MAnchester
1996
pb
276

LINS
Osman
Queen of the prisons of Greece, The
*Rainha dos cárceres da Grécia*
Frizzi, A
Dalkey Archive P: Normal IL
1995
186

LISPECTOR
Clarice
Apple in the Dark, The
*Maçã no escuro, A*
1961
Rabassa, Gregory
Texas UP
pb
378

LISPECTOR
Clarice
Apple in the Dark, The
*Maçã no escuro, A*
1961
Rabassa, Gregory
Knopf
1967

361

LISPECTOR
Clarice
Apple in the Dark, The
*Maçã no escuro, A*
1961
Rabassa, Gregory
Virago
1985
pb
378

LISPECTOR
Clarice
Apprenticeship or a book of delights, An
*Aprendizagem ou O Livro dos prazeres, Uma*
1969
Mazzara, Richard A & Parris, Lorri
Texas UP
1986
pb
126

LISPECTOR
Clarice
Besieged City, The
*Cidade sitiada*
1949
Pontiero, Giovanni
Carcanet
1999
Carcanet
1995
hb
160

LISPECTOR
Clarice
Discovering the World
*Descoberta do mundo, A*
Pontiero, G
Carcanet
1992
hb
400

LISPECTOR
Clarice
Family Ties
*Laços de família*
1960
Pontiero, G
Texas UP
1972
pb
156

LISPECTOR
Clarice
Family Ties

*Laços de família*
1960
Pontiero, G
Carcanet
1985
hb
156

LISPECTOR
Clarice
Family Ties
*Laços de família*
1960
Pontiero, G
Carcanet
1985
pb
156

LISPECTOR
Clarice
Foreign Legion, The
*Legião estrangeira, A*
1964
Pontiero, Giovanni
New Directions
1992
pb
224

LISPECTOR
Clarice
Foreign Legion, The
*Legião estrangeira, A*
1964
Pontiero, Giovanni
Carcanet
1986
hb
219

LISPECTOR
Clarice
Foreign Legion, The
*Legião estrangeira, A*
1964
Pontiero, Giovanni
Carcanet
1986
pb
219

LISPECTOR
Clarice
Hour of the Star
*Hora da estrela, A*
1977
Pontiero, Giovanni
Paladin
1987
pb
96

LISPECTOR

Clarice
**Hour of the Star**
*Hora da estrela, A*
1977
Pontiero, Giovanni
Carcanet
1992
pb
96

**LISPECTOR**
Clarice
**Hour of the Star, The**
*Hora da estrela, A*
1977
Pontiero, Giovanni
New Directions
1986
96
Carcanet
1986
hb
96

**LISPECTOR**
Clarice
**Near to the Wild Heart**
*Perto do coracão selvagem*
1944
Pontiero, Giovanni
Carcanet
1990
hb
192

**LISPECTOR**
Clarice
**Near to the Wild Heart**
*Perto do coracão selvagem*
1944
Pontiero, Giovanni
New Directions, NY
1990
192
hb

**LISPECTOR**
Clarice
**Passion according to G.H., The**
*Paixão segundo G.H., A*
1964
Minnesota UP: Minneapolis
1988
173

**LISPECTOR**
Clarice
**Selected cronicas**
*Descoberta do mundo, A*
Pontiero, G
New Directions

1996
212
hb

**LISPECTOR**
Clarice
**Soulstorm**
*Via crucis do corpo, A*
Leviton, Alexis
New Directions
1989
175

**LISPECTOR**
Clarice
**Stream of Life, The**
*Água Viva*
1973
Lowe, E. & Fitz, E.
Minnesota UP: Minneapolis
1989
79

**LOBATO**
José Bento Monteiro
**Brazilian Short Stories**
*Urupês*
Haldeman-Julius: Girard, Kansas
1925

**LUFT**
Lya
**Island of the Dead**
*Quarto Fechado, O*
1984
McLendon, CC & Craige, BJ
Georgia UP
1986
hb
112


**LUFT**
Lya
**Island of the Dead**
*Quarto Fechado, O*
1984
McLendon, CC & Craige, BJ
Georgia UP
1986
hb
106

**LUFT**
Lya
**Red House, The**
*Exílio*
1987
Pontiero, Giovanni
Carcanet
1994
hb

182
**MACHADO DE ASSIS**
Joaquim Maria
**Brazilian Tales**
Brandon
pb

**MACHADO DE ASSIS**
Joaquim Maria
**Brazilian Tales**
Brandon
pb

**MACHADO DE ASSIS**
Joaquim Maria
**Counselor Ayres' memorial**
*Memorial de Ayres*
1908
Caldwell, Helen
California U.P.
1973
pb

**MACHADO DE ASSIS**
Joaquim Maria
**Counselor Ayres' memorial**
*Memorial de Ayres*
1908
Caldwell, Helen
California U.P.
1973
hb

**MACHADO DE ASSIS**
Joaquim Maria
**Counselor Ayres' memorial**
*Memorial de Ayres*
1908
Caldwell, Helen
California U.P.
1973
pb

**MACHADO DE ASSIS**
Joaquim Maria
**Devil's Church & Other Stories, The**
*Igreja do diabo, A*
Schmitt, J. & Ishimatsu, L.
Texas UP
1977
pb
166

**MACHADO DE ASSIS**
Joaquim Maria
**Devil's Church & Other Stories, The**
*Igreja do Diabo, A*
Schmitt, J. & Ishimatsu, L.
Carcanet
1985

hb
MACHADO DE ASSIS
Joaquim Maria
Devil's Church & Other Stories, The
*Igreja do diabo, A*
Schmidt, J. & Ishimatsu, L.
Grafton
1987
pb
166

MACHADO DE ASSIS
Joaquim Maria
Dom Casmurro
*Dom Casmurro*
1900
Caldwell, Helen
California UP
1966
269

MACHADO DE ASSIS
Joaquim Maria
Dom Casmurro
*Dom Casmurro*
1900
Caldwell, Helen
W.H.Allen
1953

MACHADO DE ASSIS
Joaquim Maria
Dom Casmurro. (A novel)
*Dom Casmurro*
Helen Caldwell
W.H. Allen
1953
237

MACHADO DE ASSIS
Joaquim Maria
Dom Casmurro. (A novel)
*Dom Casmurro*
Helen Caldwell
New York, Noonday Press
1953
283

MACHADO DE ASSIS
Joaquim Maria
Dom Casmurro. (A novel)
*Dom Casmurro*
John Gledson
OUP NY
1997
258
OUP, Oxford
1997
237

MACHADO DE ASSIS

Joaquim Maria
Dom Casmurro
*Dom Casmurro*
1900
Caldwell, Helen
Noonday
1953

MACHADO DE ASSIS
Joaquim Maria
Dom Casmurro
*Dom Casmurro*
1900
Scott-Buccleugh, R.L.
Owen
1992
hb
216

MACHADO DE ASSIS
Joaquim Maria
Epitaph of A Small Winner
*Memorias posthumas de Braz Cubas*
William L. Grossman
New York, Noonday Press
1952
223

MACHADO DE ASSIS
Joaquim Maria
Epitaph of a Small Winner
*Memórias posthumas de Braz Cubas*
William L. Grossman
New York, Noonday Press
1956
223

MACHADO DE ASSIS
Joaquim Maria
Epitaph of a Small Winner
*Memórias póstumas de Brás cubas*
1881
Grossman, William
Hogarth Press
1985
hb

MACHADO DE ASSIS
Joaquim Maria
Epitaph of a Small Winner
*Memórias póstumas de Brás cubas*
1881
Grossman, William
Vintage
1991
pb

MACHADO DE ASSIS

Joaquim Maria
Epitaph of a Small Winner
*Memórias póstumas de Brás cubas*
1881
Grossman, William
Bloomsbury
1997
pb
209

MACHADO DE ASSIS
Joaquim Maria
Esau and Jacob
*Esaú e Jacó*
1904
Caldwell, Helen
California UP
1965
287

MACHADO DE ASSIS
Joaquim Maria
Esau and Jacob
*Esaú e Jacó*
1904
Caldwell, Helen
Owen
1966
hb
287

MACHADO DE ASSIS
Joaquim Maria
Esau and Jacob
*Esaú e Jacó*
1904
Elizabeth Lowe
Oxford UP: NY
2000
368
Oxford UP:Oxford
2000
368

MACHADO DE ASSIS
Joaquim Maria
Hand and the Glove, The
*Mão e a luva, A*
1874
Bagby, Albert Ian Jr.
Kentucky UP: Lexington
1970
116

MACHADO DE ASSIS
Joaquim Maria
Helena
*Helena*
1876
Caldwell, Helen
California UP
1984

MACHADO DE ASSIS
Joaquim Maria
Helena
*Helena*
1876
Caldwell, Helen
California UP
1984
hb
197

MACHADO DE ASSIS
Joaquim Maria
Helena
*Helena*
1876
Caldwell, Helen
California UP
1984
pb
197

MACHADO DE ASSIS
Joaquim Maria
Heritage of Quincas Borba, The
*Quincas Borba*
1891
Wilson, Clotilde
Allen & Unwin
1954
pb

MACHADO DE ASSIS
Joaquim Maria
Philosopher or Dog?
*Quincas Borba*
Clotilde Wilson
New York, Noonday Press
1956
271

MACHADO DE ASSIS
Joaquim Maria
Philosopher or Dog?
*Quincas Borba*
1891
Wilson, Clotilde
Farrar Strauss
1992
pb
288

MACHADO DE ASSIS
Joaquim Maria
Philosopher or Dog?
*Quincas Borba*
1891
Wilson, Clotilde
W.H.Allen
1954
pb
288

MACHADO DE ASSIS
Joaquim Maria
Posthumous Memoirs of Bras Cubas: a novel
*Memórias póstumas de Brás Cubas*
1904
Gregory Rabassa
Oxford UP: NY
1997
256
Oxford UP: London
1997
256

MACHADO DE ASSIS
Joaquim Maria
Psychiatrist and other stories, The
Grossman, W. & Caldwell, H.
California UP, Berkeley
1963
147

MACHADO DE ASSIS
Joaquim Maria
Psychiatrist and other stories, The
Grossman, W. & Caldwell, H.
Owen
1963

MACHADO DE ASSIS
Joaquim Maria
Quincas Borba
*Quincas Borba*
1891
Gregory Rabassa
OUP: NY
1998
OUP: Oxford
1998
pb
290

MACHADO DE ASSIS
Joaquim Maria
Wager: Aires' Journal
*Memorial de Aires*
1908
Scott-Buccleuch, R.L.
Dufour Editions
1990
Owen
1990
hb
165

MACHADO DE ASSIS
Joaquim Maria
What went on at the Baroness'
Helen Caudwell
Magpie P.,Santa Monica, CA
1963

MACHADO DE ASSIS
Joaquim Maria
Yayá Garcia
*Iaiá Garcia*
1878
Scott-Buccleuch, R.L.
Owen
1976
hb
220

MELO
Patricia
In praise of lies
*Elogio da mentira*
Landers, Clifford E.
Bloomsbury
1999
187

MELO
Patricia
Killer
*O Matador*
Landers, Clifford E.
Ecco P
1997
217

MIRANDA
Ana
Bay of All Saints and Every Conceivable Sin
*Boca do Inferno*
1989
Pontiero, Giovanni
Viking: NY
1991
305
Harvill
1992
hb
305

MIRANDA
Ana
Bay of All Saints and Every Conceivable Sin
*Boca do Inferno*
1989
Pontiero, Giovanni
Harvill
1992
pb

MONTELLO
José

Coronation Quay
*Cais da Sagração*
1971
Henderson, Myriam
Rex Collings
1975
pb
266
NOLL
João Gilberto
Hotel Atlantico
*Hotel Atlântico, Harmada*
1989,1993
David Treece
Boulevatrd: dist. SBS, Seattle
1997
151
Boulevard: Oxford
1997
151
NUNES
Lygia Bojunga
My friend the painter
*Meu amigo pintor*
Giovanni Pontiero
Viking: NY
1991
305
OLINTO
Antônio
Copacabana
*Copacabana*
Parker, John
London
1980
OLINTO
Antônio
Dancer's Furniture, The
*Móveis da bailarina, Os*
Benson, Constance
Humanis: NY
1987
OLINTO
Antônio
King of Ketu, The
*Rei de Keto, O*
Chappell, Richard
Rex Collings
1987
281
OLINTO
Antônio
Water House, The
*Casa de Água, A*
1969
Heapy, Dorothy
Carroll: NY

1985
410
Rex Collings
1970
410
OLINTO
Antônio
Water House, The
*Casa de Água, A*
1969
Heapy, Dorothy
Nelson: Walton-on-Thames
1982
410
PEIXOTO
Afrânio
Threshold
*Fronteira*
Reggio, Tona & Edward A
Franklin Pubs: Philadelphia
1975
PENNA
Cornelio
Threshold
*Fronteira*
1935
Riggio, Tona & Riggio, Edward
Franklin: Philadelphia
1975
PEREIRA
Antonio Olavo
Marcore
*Marcoré*
1957
Hower, A. & Saunders, J.
Texas UP
1970
234
PIÑON
Nélida
Caetanas's Sweet Song
*Doce cançao de Caetana, A*
Lane, Helen
Knopf
1992
401
PIÑON
Nélida
Republic of Dreams, The
*Republica dos sonhos, A*
Lane, Helen
Knopf
1989
663
QUEIROZ
Dinah Silveira de
Christ's Memorial

*Eu, venho*
1974
Prado, Isabel do
Sel P: London
1978
214
QUEIROZ
Dinah Silveira de
Women of Brazil, The
*A Muralha*
1970
King, Roberta
Rex Collings
1978
112
QUEIROZ
Rachel de
Dora, Doralina
*Dora, Doralina*
Loos, Dorothy Scott
Avon
pb
QUEIROZ
Rachel de
Dora, Doralina
*Dora, Doralina*
Loos, Dorothy Scott
Avon
1986
pb
QUEIROZ
Rachel de
Three Marias, The
*Tres Marias, As*
1939
Ellison, Fred P.
Texas UP
1963
178
RAMOS
Graciliano
Anguish
*Angustia*
1936
Kaplin, L.C.
Greenwood P
1972
RAMOS
Graciliano
Barren Lives
*Vidas Secas*
1938
Dimmick, Ralph E.
Texas UP
1965
hb
RAMOS

Graciliano
**Barren Lives**
*Vidas Secas*
Dimmick, Ralph E.
Texas UP
1965
pb

RAMOS
Graciliano
**Childhood**
*Infância*
1945
de Oliveira, Celso
Owen
1979
174

RAMOS
Graciliano
**Jail Memoirs**
*Memórias do cárcere*
1953
Colchie, Thomas
Evans: NY
1974

RAMOS
Graciliano
**São Bernardo**
*Sâo Bernardo*
1934
Scott-Buccleuch, R.L.
Taplinger NY
Owen
1975
hb
156

RAWET
Samuel
**Prophet, The & Other Stories**
**(Jewish Latin America Series)**
Nelson H. Vieira
University of New Mexico Press
112

REGO
José Lins do
**Plantation Boy**
*Menino de Engenho*
1932
Baum, Emmi
Knopf: NY
1966

REGO
José Lins do
**Pureza**
*Pureza*
1937
Marion, Lucie
Hutchinson: London
1948

RESENDE
Otto Lara
**Inspector of Orphans, The**
*Braço direito, O*
1963
Cravinho, Anne
Deutsch: London
1968

REY
Marcos
**Memoirs of a gigolo**
*Memórias de um gigolo*
1968
Landers, Clifford E.
Avon
1987
217

RIBEIRO
Darcy
**Maira**
*Maira*
1978
Goodland, E.H. & Colchie, T.
Vintage
1984
hb
353

RIBEIRO
Darcy
**Maira**
*Maíra*
1978
Goodland, E.H. & Colchie, T.
Picador
1985
pb
353

RIBEIRO
Edgard Telles
**I Would Have Loved Him If I Had Not Killed Him**
*Criado Mudo*
Neves, M A
St. Martin's : NY
1994
208

RIBEIRO
Joâo Ubaldo
**Invincible Memory, An**
*Viva o povo brasileiro*
1984
Author
Harper & Row: NY
1989
hb
504

RIBEIRO
Joâo Ubaldo
**Invincible Memory, An**
*Viva o povo brasileiro*
1984
Author
Faber
1991
hb
504

RIBEIRO
Joâo Ubaldo
**Invincible Memory, An**
*Viva o povo brasileiro*
1984
Author
Faber
1991
pb

RIBEIRO
Joâo Ubaldo
**Lizard's Smile, The**
*Sorriso do lagarto*
Atheneum: NY
1995
hb
355

RIBEIRO
Joâo Ubaldo
**Lizard's Smile, The**
*Sorriso do lagarto*
Deutsch: London
1995
hb
355

RIBEIRO
Joâo Ubaldo
**Sergeant Getulio**
*Sargento Getúlio*
1971
Author
Houghton Mifflin: Boston
1978
146

RIBEIRO
Joâo Ubaldo
**Sergeant Getulio**
*Sargento Getúlio*
1971
Author
Deutsch: London
1994
pb
146

**RIBEIRO**
João Ubaldo
Sergeant Getulio
*Sargento Getúlio*
1971
Author
Faber: London
1986
146

**RIBEIRO**
Stella Carr
Sambaqui: a novel of Pre-history
*Homem do Sambaqui, O*
1975
Heuvel, Claudia van de
Avon
1987

**ROSA** see **GUIMARÃES ROSA, João**

**RUBIÃO**
Murilo
Ex-magician and other stories, The
*Dragões e outros contos, Os*
1965
Colchie, Thomas
Harper
1979
133

**RORIZ**
Aydano
Diamonds Are Forgiving
*Os Diamantes não são eternos*
Prospect Press
1999
239

**SABINO**
Fernando
Time to meet, A
*Encontro marcado, O*
1956
Procter, John
Souvenir
1967
hb

**SABINO**
Fernando
Time to meet, A
*Encontro marcado, O*
1956
Procter, John
Panther
1967
pb

319
**SALES**
Herbert
Werewolf and other stories, The
*Lobisomem e outros contos folcloricos*
1970
Goddard, Richard
Rex Collings
1978
112

**SALES**
Herberto
Fruit of thy Womb, The
*O fruto do vosso ventre*
Michael Fody
Wyvern: Bringsty
1982
185

**SALES**
Herberto
Werewolf and other stories, The
*Lobisomem e outros contos folcloricos*
1970
Goddard, Richard
Rex Collings
1978
112

**SANTARENO**
Bernardo
Promise, The
Nelson H. Viera
Center for Portuguese & Brazilian Studies: rovidence, R.I.
107

**SANTIAGO**
Silviano
Stella Manhattan
*Stella Manhattan*
1985
Yudice, George
Columbia UP: NY
1990
212

**SANTIAGO**
Silviano
Stella Manhattan
*Stella Manhattan*
1985
Yudice, George
Duke UP: dist AUPG
1995
hb
212

**SANTIAGO**
Silviano
Stella Manhattan
*Stella Manhattan*
1985
Yudice, George
Duke UP: Durham, NC
1994
212
Duke UP: dist AUPG
1995
pb
212

**SARNEY**
José
Tales of Rain & Sunlight
*Noites das Aguas*
1969
Hallam, Vera
Wyvern: Bringsty, Worcs.
1986
143

**SCLIAR**
Moacyr
Ballad of the False Messiah, The
*Balada do falso Messias*
1976
Ballantine
1987
pb
89

**SCLIAR**
Moacyr
Carnival of the Animals
*Carnaval dos animais, O*
1968
Giacomelli, Eloah F.
Ballantine
1985
pb

**SCLIAR**
Moacyr
Centaur in the Garden, The
*Centauro no jardim, O*
1980
Neves, Margaret A.
Ballantine
1988
pb

**SCLIAR**
Moacyr
Centaur in the Garden, The
*Centauro no jardim, O*
1980
Neves, Margaret A.
Available P: NY

SCLIAR
Moacyr
Enigmatic eye, The
*Olho enigmatico, O*
Eloah F. Giacomelli
Ballantine
1989
pb
100

SCLIAR
Moacyr
Enigmatic eye, The
*Olho enigmatico, O*
Eloah F. Giacomelli
Available P: NY
1989
100

SCLIAR
Moacyr
Gods Of Raquel
*Deuses de Raquel, Os*
1975
Ballantine
1986
pb
107

SCLIAR
Moacyr
Max and the cats: a novel
*Max e os felinos*
Eloah F. Giacomelli
Ballantine
1989
pb
99

SCLIAR
Moacyr
One-Man Army, The
*Exército da um homem só, O*
1973
Giacomelli, Eloah F.
Ballantine:NY
1986
pb
154

SCLIAR
Moacyr
Strange Nation of Rafael Mendes, The
*Estranha nação de Rafael Mendes*
Giacomelli, Eloah F.
Ballantine
1989
pb
301

SCLIAR
Moacyr
Strange Nation of Rafael Mendes, The
*Estranha nação de Rafael Mendes*
Giacomelli, Eloah F.
Harmony Books: NY
1988
301

SCLIAR
Moacyr
Volunteers, The
*Voluntários, Os*
Ballantine
1988
pb
152

SCLIAR
Moacyr
Volunteers, The
*Voluntários, Os*
Available P: NY
1988
151

SETÚBAL
Paulo de Oliveira
Domitila: the romance of the emperor's mistress
*Marquesa de Santos, A*
Hollingsworth, M R
Coward-McCann
1930
324

SOARES
Jô
A samba for Sherlock
*Xangô de Baker Street*
Landers, Clifford E.

SOUZA
Márcio de
Death Squeeze
*Condolência, A*
Watson, Ellen
Avon
1992
321

SOUZA
Márcio de
Emperor of the Amazon
*Galvez, Imperador do Acre*
1976
Colchie, Thomas
Avon
1977

pb
190

SOUZA
Márcio de
Emperor of the Amazon
*Galvez, Imperador do Acre*
1976
Colchie, Thomas
Sphere/Abacus
1982
pb
189

SOUZA
Márcio de
Lost World ll - the End of the Third World
*Fim do Terceiro Mundo, O*
Santamaria, Lana
Avon
1993
362

SOUZA
Márcio de
Mad Maria
*Mad Maria*
1980
Colchie, Thomas
Avon
1986
pb

SOUZA
Márcio de
Order of the day. An unidentified flying opus., The
*Ordem do dia, A*
1983
Colchie, Thomas
Avon
1986
223

STEEN
Edla van
Bag of Stories, A
George, David Sanderson
Latin American Literary Review P
1991
pb

STEEN
Edla van
Bag of Stories, A
George, David Sanderson
Latin American Literary Review
P: Pittsburgh, PA
1991
174

STEEN

Edla van
Early Mourning (Discoveries)
George, David Sanderson
Latin American Literary Review P
1997
pb
150

STEEN
Edla van
Village of the Ghost Bells
*Corações Mordidos*
George, David Sanderson
Texas UP
1991
197

STEEN
Edla van
Village of the Ghost Bells
*Corações Mordidos*
George, David Sanderson
Texas UP
1991
197

TAUNAY
Viscount A de
Inocencia
*Inocência*
1872
Chamberlain, Henrietta
Macmillan: NY
1945
209

TAUNAY
Viscount A de
Inocencia
*Inocência*
1872
?
Heath: London
1921

TELLES
Lygia Fagundes
Girl in the Photograph, The
*Meninas, As*
1973
Neves, Margaret A.
Avon
1982

TELLES
Lygia Fagundes
Marble Dance, The
*Ciranda de Pedra*
1954
Neves, Margaret A.
Avon
1986

184
TELLES
Lygia Fagundes
Tigrela & other stories
*Seminário dos Ratos*
1977
Neves, Margaret A.
Avon
1986
152

TORRES
Antônio
Blues for a Lost Childhood
*Balada da infância perdida*
1986
Parker, J
Readers' International: Columbia,
LA
Readers' International: London
1989
hb
202

TORRES
Antônio
Blues for a Lost Childhood
*Balada da infância perdida*
1986
Parker, J
Readers' International
1989
pb

TORRES
Antônio
Land, The
*Essa Terra*
1976
Neves, M.A.
Readers' International
1987
hb
136

TORRES
Antônio
Land, The
*Essa Terra*
1976
Neves, M.A.
Readers' International: contact publisher.to
1987
pb

TREVISAN
Dalton
Vampire of Curtiba & other stories, The
*Vampiro de Curtiba, O*
1965

Rabassa, Gregory
Knopf
1972
267

VASCONCELOS
José Mauro de
My sweet-orange tree
*Meu pé de laranja lima*
1968
Miller, Edgar H. (Jr.)
Knopf
1970

VASCONCELOS
José Mauro de
My sweet-orange tree
*Meu pé de laranja lima*
1968
Miller, Edgar H. (Jr.)
M. Joseph: London
1971

VASCONCELOS
José Mauro de
My sweet-orange tree
*Meu pé de laranja lima*
1968
Miller, Edgar H. (Jr.)
Hutchinson: London
1983
166

VEIGA
José
Misplaced Machine, The
*Máquina extraviada*
1968
Bird, Pamela G.
Knopf
1970
141

VEIGA
José
Three Trials of Manirema, The
*Hora dos ruminantes, A*
1966
Bird, Pamela G.
Knopf
1970
154

VEIGA
José
Three Trials of Manirema, The
*Hora dos ruminantes, A*
1966
Bird, Pamela G.
Owen
1979

154
**VERÍSSIMO**
Érico
Consider the Lilies of the Field
*Olhai os lírios do campo*
1938
Karnoff, Jean
Macmillan
1947

**VERÍSSIMO**
Érico
Consider the Lilies of the Field
*Olhai os lírios do campo*
1938
Karnoff, Jean
Greenwood: NY
1969

**VERÍSSIMO**
Érico
Consider the Lilies of the Field
*Olhai os lírios do campo*
1938
Karnoff, Jean
Greenwood?: NY
1969
371

**VERÍSSIMO**
Érico
Crossroads And Destinies
*Caminhos cruzados*
1937
Kaplan, L.C.
Arco
1958
373

**VERÍSSIMO**
Érico
Crossroads and destinies
*Caminhos cruzados*
1935
Kaplan, L.C.
Macmillan
1943
373

**VERÍSSIMO**
Érico
Crossroads and destinies
*Caminhos cruzados*
1935
Kaplan, L.C.
Greenwood: NY
1969
373

**VERÍSSIMO**
Érico
Crossroads and destinies
*Caminhos cruzados*
1935
Kaplan, L.C.
Arco: London
1956

**VERÍSSIMO**
Érico
Evil In The Night
*Noite*
L.L. Barrett
Greenwich Conn, Fawcett Publs
1956
142

**VERÍSSIMO**
Érico
His Excellency, the Ambassador
*Senhor Ambaixador, O*
1965
Barrett, Linton & Marie
Macmillan
1967
439

**VERÍSSIMO**
Érico
Night
*Noite*
L.L. Barett
New York, Macmillan
1958
166

**VERÍSSIMO**
Érico
Night
*Noite*
L.L. Barrett
Arco
1958
166

**VERÍSSIMO**
Érico
Night
*Noite*
1954
Barrett, Linton L.
Macmillan
1956
166

**VERÍSSIMO**
Érico
Night
*Noite*
1954
Barrett, Linton L.
Arco: London
1956

**VERÍSSIMO**
Érico
Rest Is Silence, The
*O Resto é silêncio*
1950
Kaplan, L.C.
Arco
1958
485

**VERÍSSIMO**
Érico
Rest is Silence, The
*O Resto é silêncio*
1953
Kaplan, L.C.
Macmillan
1946
485

**VERÍSSIMO**
Érico
Rest is Silence, The
*O Resto é silêncio*
1953
Kaplan, L.C.
Greenwood
1969
485

**VERÍSSIMO**
Érico
Rest is Silence, The
*O Resto é silêncio*
1953
Kaplan, L.C.
Arco: London
1956

**VERÍSSIMO**
Érico
Time And The Wind
*O tempo e o vento*
1950
L.L. Barrett
Arco Publications
1954
624

**VERÍSSIMO**
Érico
Time and the Wind
*Tempo e o vento, O*
1949
Barrett, Linton L.
Macmillan
1951
624

**VERÍSSIMO**
Érico

Time and the Wind
*Tempo e o vento, O*
1949
Barrett, Linton L.
Greenwood: NY
624
## VERÍSSIMO
Érico
Time and the Wind
*Tempo e o vento, O*
1949
Barrett, Linton L.
Arco: London
1954
624

'a brilliant idea, well executed'
> — *The Good Book Guide*

'accessible and entertaining'
> — *Traveller's Literary Companion*

Babel Guide to Italian Fiction in Translation
ISBN 1899460004 £9.95/$14.95
Babel Guide to the Fiction of Portugal, Brazil & Africa in Translation
ISBN 1899460055 £9.95/$14.95
Babel Guide to French Fiction in Translation
ISBN 1899460101 £12.95/$18.95
Babel Guide to German Fiction in Translation
ISBN 1899460209 £12.95/$18.95
Babel Guide to Jewish Fiction
ISBN 189946025 X £12.95/$18.95
Babel Guide to Scandinavian Fiction in Translation
ISBN 1899460 30 6 £12.95/$18.95
Babel Guide to Dutch and Flemish Fiction in Translation
ISBN 1899460 80 2 £12.95/$18.95
Babel Guide to Hungarian Literature in Translation
ISBN 1899460 85 3 £12.95/$18.95
Babel Guide to Brazilian Fiction in Translation
ISBN 1899460 70 5 £12.95/$18.95
Babel Guide to Modern Greek Literature in Translation
ISBN 1899460 35 7 £12.95/$18.95

[Spanish, Welsh, Latin American, Yiddish, Russian, Arab, Japanese, Indian Subcontinent, Chinese and other Babel Guides to be announced.]

Available in bookshops or from the publisher, post and packing free in the European Union, elsewhere please add 10%, US$ or UK£ cheques/eurocheques accepted. BOULEVARD 71 Lytton Road Oxford OX4 3NY 01865 712931

Boulevard Books are distributed in the **UK & Europe** by Drake International, Market House, Market Place, Deddington, Oxford 0X15 0SE tel 01869 338240 fax 338310 info@drakeint.co.uk www.drakeint.co.uk

and in the **USA & Canada** by ISBS
5804 NE Hassio St, Portland, Oregon 97213-3644
tel 00 1 503 287 3093 fax 280 8832 info@isbs.com